Mrs Jane C. Loudon

Instructions in

GARDENING

FOR

LADIES

Gladiolus

Mrs Jane C. Loudon

Instructions in

GARDENING
FOR
LADIES

CONSTABLE

Constable & Robinson Ltd
55-56 Russell Square
London WC1B 4HP

A copy of the British Library Cataloguing in Publication Data is
available from the British Library

ISBN 978-1-47210-648-3

Designed and typeset by Design 23, London
Printed in the UK

MIX
Paper from
responsible sources
FSC
www.fsc.org   FSC® C018072

CONTENTS

Sphaerospora, Synnotia

FOREWORD

Jane Austen and the Brontë sisters, had their lives dovetailed a little more neatly with that of Jane Loudon, need have looked no further to find the inspiration for a new heroine to grace the pages of their literary endeavours. Loudon's life was packed with the kind of drama, glamour and heartache that would surely turn any novel into a bestseller. As passionate and independent as Charlotte Brontë's Jane Eyre; as feisty and intelligent as Jane Austen's Elizabeth Bennet in *Pride and Prejudice*, Jane Loudon sadly had as many woes to endure as either of those fictional characters.

Born in Birmingham in 1807, Jane was the daughter of Thomas Webb, a wealthy industrialist. When she was only 12 years old, Jane's mother died and she and her father then embarked on a year-long odyssey around Europe, during which she studied foreign languages, enjoying the sort of cultural experiences which, when young men made similar educational trips, had become known as 'The Grand Tour.' All was not well, however, when they returned to their home at Edgbaston. Thomas Webb's business was failing and speculative investments that he made to try to bolster his finances left him in ruins. He died in 1824, his fortune having evaporated, forcing Jane to find a way to support herself. This she did by writing, first publishing a book of prose and verse, then following that with a far more outlandish effort.

When Jane first met John Claudius Loudon, the man who was to become her husband, they must have seemed an unlikely match. He had asked to be introduced to the author of a science

fiction horror novel called *The Mummy!: Or a Tale of the Twenty-
Second Century*. Loudon was from Scottish farming stock and
had made a name for himself as a landscape architect and expert
botanist. With his passion for all things agricultural, Loudon
was especially interested in *The Mummy!* author's futuristic
ideas about a steam-driven plough which, when the tale was
first published in 1827, preceded the actual development of the
steam plough by more than twenty years. The book also featured
buildings with air conditioning and an idea similar to the modern-
day Internet. When the meeting was arranged through a mutual
friend in February 1830, Loudon expected that the author would
be a man and was pleasantly surprised to find himself greeting an
attractive 23-year-old woman. Jane had written the novel under
an assumed name, deciding that it stood more chance of being
taken seriously if the author was thought to be a man.

She later wrote about how she recognised an attraction
between Loudon and herself from the very first time they met,
and it was an aquaintance that swiftly developed into romance.
They were married only seven months later. Just as Austen and
the Brontës would have wished, however, Jane was not destined
to live happily ever after. At 47 years of age, John was a good
deal older than her, Jane's affection for him perhaps reflecting
the closeness of her relationship with her father, and he was in
poor health. He had been plagued with arthritis from a young
age, walking with a limp and, when an operation to mend his
badly broken right arm had gone disastrously wrong, the entire
limb had to be amputated at the shoulder. He had been forced
to teach himself to write and to draw botanical specimens using

his left hand. That goes a long way towards demonstrating the remarkable Mr Loudon's strength of character, which drove him on to produce an impressive body of work despite his physical frailty.

If you marry a man whose family were farmers and who studied botany at university, a man who has written books and established magazines devoted to gardening and horticulture, a man whose life's work has been to create green spaces in Britain's cities, promoting revolutionary town planning to bring some healthy colour into the lives of downtrodden factory workers, you have to be the kind of girl who is prepared to learn a bit about gardening. Jane Webb did more than learn just a bit. She listened to everything that her husband had to tell her, and worked in the large garden they established at their house in Porchester Terrace in London. Jane described the house as having a stile at the bottom of their extensive rear garden that led onto a field where cows grazed. Nowadays, Porchester Terrace in Bayswater is very much part of Central London, with open countryside rather a long way off.

In 1832, the couple had a daughter, Agnes. Jane worked all the way through her pregnancy, helping John as his secretary, taking notes and continuing to expand her own knowledge of gardening. She regularly attended Royal Horticultural Society lectures given by John Lindley, who had worked with her husband on his *Encyclopedia of Plants* but was quickly coming to the conclusion that the scientific approach to horticulture adopted by her husband and his contemporaries was dauntingly inaccessible to most budding gardeners. Although they wanted to popularise the idea of gardening, the very people that they hoped to encourage lacked the education to tackle even the names of some of the new species of exotic garden plants that were being imported to, and propagated in, nurseries all over Britain. Foremost amongst these aspiring cultivators were women, and women from anything other than farm workers' families were not used to performing manual labour in the great outdoors. Even middle class women with something of an education knew little about how to grow garden plants successfully, and previously they would have been positively discouraged from attempting any kind of hard work in the garden. Sitting in the shade on a summer's day was considered strenuous enough for most young ladies. The lack of knowledge and the unhelpful attitude were things that Jane decided she could help to remedy.

When production of John Loudon's mammoth book, *Arboretum et Fruticetum Britannicum*, a record of all of the trees and shrubs growing in Great Britain, left the family on the verge of financial ruin, Jane decided to put her writing skills to good use once again. She produced the *Young Ladies' Book of Botany* in 1838 and followed that with *Gardening for Ladies* in 1840. The original version of *Gardening for Ladies* included practical illustrations, many of which are reproduced in this edition, but did not include the drawings of flowers that appear in this book. These actually come from a later series of Jane Loudon books: *The Ladies' Flower Garden* (produced in four volumes between 1840 and 1848) and *The Ladies' Companion to the Flower Garden* (1841). Among her other talents, Jane was a self-taught artist and all of the illustrations, lovingly coloured in their original guise, were her own work.

Gardening for Ladies, the full title of which was *Instructions in Gardening for Ladies*, took its readers through the basics of digging the soil to more complex procedures such as taking cuttings and grafting plants. It sold an incredible 200,000 copies, but the income generated by it, and Jane's other books, could not sustain the family for long. John's health continued to deteriorate, exacerbated by his punishing workload and financial worries, until he succumbed to lung cancer two weeks before Christmas in 1843. Such was her concern for him as he paced the floor that night, that Jane later wrote, 'I perceived a change taking place in his countenance, and I had just time to clasp my arms around him, to save him falling, when his head sank upon my shoulder and he was no more.'

Once again Jane was forced to provide for herself, and for her daughter, earning an income from writing and working as an editor on gardening magazines. Jane was awarded a small annual pension from the Civil List, but struggled financially for the rest of her days. Her books and magazines, the original editions of which are now very rare and highly valued, created controversy at the time, some elements of the male-dominated gardening circles finding it difficult to accept that what they regarded as a mere woman should have the effrontery to intrude upon their area of expertise. That, without a doubt, would have been exactly the way that Austen or the Brontës would have wanted it – the plucky heroine standing her ground to the last.

Jane, her name sometimes styled Jane C. Loudon just as her husband was John C. Loudon, and sometimes Jane Webb Loudon, died in July 1858 at the age of 51.

INTRODUCTION

WHEN I married Mr. Loudon, it is scarcely possible to imagine any person more completely ignorant than I was, of every thing relating to plants and gardening; and, as may be easily imagined, I found every one about me so well acquainted with the subject, that I was soon heartily ashamed of my ignorance. My husband, of course, was quite as anxious to teach me as I was to learn, and it is the result of his instruction, that I now (after ten years experience of their efficacy) wish to make public for the benefit of others.

I do this, because I think books intended for professional gardeners are seldom suitable to the wants of amateurs. It is so very difficult for a person who has been acquainted with a subject all his life, to imagine the state of ignorance in which a person is who knows nothing of it, that adepts often find it impossible to communicate the knowledge they possess. Thus, though it may at first sight appear presumptuous in me to attempt to teach an art of which for three-fourths of my life I was perfectly ignorant, it is in fact that very circumstance which is one of my chief qualifications for the task. Having been a full-grown pupil myself, I know the wants of others in a similar situation; and having never been satisfied without knowing the reason for every thing I was told to do, I am able to impart these reasons to others. Thus my readers will be able to judge for themselves, and to adapt their practice to the circumstances in which they may be placed.

In the present edition, the whole work has been carefully revised and improved; and several considerable and important additions have been made.

I have only to add, that I have spared no pains to render the work as perfect as I could make it. The engravings have been made here from drawings of specimens previously prepared, and I can therefore vouch for their accuracy.

J. W. L.

Bayswater, Dec. 16, 1840.

Babiana

CHAPTER I

STIRRING THE SOIL

Digging

Every one knows that the first operation of the gardener, whether a new garden is to be made, or merely an old one re-planted, is to dig the ground; though but comparatively few persons are aware why this is so essentially necessary to be done. When a piece of rough ground is to be taken into cultivation, and a garden made where there was none before, the use of digging is obvious enough; as the ground requires to be levelled, and divided by walks, and thrown up into beds, to give it the shape and appearance of a garden, which could not be done without stirring the soil: but why the beds in an old garden should be always dug or forked over, before they are re-planted, is quite another question, and one that requires some consideration to answer.

When any soil, except sand or loose gravel, remains unstirred for a length of time, it becomes hard, and its particles adhere so firmly together as not to be separated without manual force. It is quite clear that when soil is in this state, it is unfit for the reception of seeds; as the tender roots of the young plants will not be able to penetrate it without great difficulty, and neither air nor water can reach them in sufficient quantity to make them thrive. When a seed is put into the ground, it is the warmth

and moisture by which it is surrounded that make it vegetate.
It first swells, and the skin with which it is covered cracks and
peels off; then two shoots issue from the vital knot, (a point
easily discoverable in large seeds,) one of which descends and
is called the root, while the other ascends to form the leaves,
stem, flowers and fruit.

This is what is meant by the germination of the seed, and this
may be effected by the aid of heat and moisture alone, as is done
with mustard and cress, when raised on a wet flannel in a saucer.
But plants raised in this manner cannot be of long duration; as,
though they will live for a short time on the albumen contained
in the seed, (on which they feed, as the chicken does on the
nourishment contained in the egg,) this is soon exhausted, and
the plant will die if not supplied with fresh food, which it can
only obtain by means of the root. Thus, the root is necessary,
not only to form a base to support the plant and to keep it
upright, but to supply it with food; and nature has given it a
tendency to bury itself in the ground, not only to enable the
plant to take a firm hold of the soil, but to preserve the root in
a fitting state for absorbing food, which it can only do when it
is kept warm, moist, and secluded from the light.

The manner in which the root is fitted for the purposes for
which it was designed, affords an admirable illustration of the
care and wisdom displayed by the Great Creator in all his works.
In nature nothing is superfluous, and yet everything has been
provided for. It has been already observed, that the two principal
uses of the root are to give the plant a firm hold of the ground,
and to supply it with food. For the first purpose the root either

spreads so widely through the surface soil as to form a sufficient base for the height of the plant, or it descends a sufficient depth into the earth to steady the part above ground; and in either case the growth of the plant is wisely and wonderfully proportioned to the strength of the support which the root affords it.

For the second purpose, that of supplying the plant with nourishment, the root divides at the extremity of each shoot into numerous fibres or fibrils, each furnished at its extremity with a spongiole or spongy substance, which affords the only means the plant possesses of absorbing the moisture necessary for its support. It is thus quite clear, that every thing that tends to nourish and increase the growth of the root, must contribute to the health and vigour of the rest of the plant; and that no plant can thrive, the root of which is cramped in its growth, or weakened for want of nourishment. This being allowed, it is evident that the first step towards promoting the growth of any plant is to provide a fitting receptacle for the root; and this is done by pulverizing the ground in which the seed is to be sown, so as to render it in a fit state for the roots to penetrate it easily. Thus they will neither be checked in their growth for want of room, nor be obliged to waste their strength in overcoming unnecessary obstacles; such as twining themselves round a stone, or trying to force their way through a hard clod of earth. The second point of affording the root abundance of nourishment may also be obtained by pulverizing the ground; as pulverisation, by admitting the rain to percolate slowly through the soil, affords a proper and equitable supply of food to the spongioles, without suffering the surplus water to remain so long around the roots, as to be in danger of rotting them.

These then are the reasons why it may be laid down as a general rule, that all ground should be stirred before seeds are sown in it; but there are other reasons which operate only partially, and are yet almost as necessary to be attended to. When manure is applied, the ground is generally well dug, in order to mix the manure intimately with the soil: and when the soil appears worn out, or poisoned with excrementitious matter, from the same kind of plants being too long grown in it, it is trenched; that is, the upper or surface soil is taken off by spadefuls and laid on one side, and the bottom or sub-soil is taken out to a certain depth previously agreed on, and laid in another heap. The surface soil is then thrown into the bottom of the trench, and the sub-soil laid on the surface, and thus a completely new and fresh soil is offered to the plants. These partial uses of digging should, however, always be applied with great caution, as in some cases manure does better laid on the surface, so that its juices only may drain into the ground, than when it is intimately mixed with the soil; and there are cases when, from the sub-soil being of an inferior quality, trenching must be manifestly injurious. Reason and experience are, in these cases, as in most others, the best guides.

The uses of digging having been thus explained, it is now necessary to say something of its practice, and particularly of its applicability to ladies. It must be confessed that digging appears at first sight a very laborious employment, and one peculiarly unfitted to small and delicately formed hands and feet; but, by a little attention to the principles of mechanics and the laws of motion, the labour may be much simplified and rendered comparatively easy. The operation of digging, as performed by a gardener, consists in thrusting the iron part of the spade, which acts as a wedge, perpendicularly into the ground by the application of the foot, and then using the long handle as a lever, to raise up the loosened earth and turn it over. The quantity of earth thus raised is called a spitful, and the gardener, when he has turned it, chops it to break the clods, with the sharp edge of his spade, and levels it with the back. During the whole operation, the gardener holds the cross part of the handle of the spade in his right-hand, while he grasps the smooth round lower part of the handle in his left, to assist him in raising the earth and turning it, sliding his left hand backwards and forwards along the handle as he may find it necessary.

This is the common mode of digging, and it certainly appears to require considerable strength in the foot to force the spade into the ground,-the arms, to raise it when loaded with the earth that is to be turned over,-and in the hands, to grasp the handle. But it must be remembered that all operations that are effected rapidly by the exertion of great power, may be effected slowly by the exertion of very little power, if that comparatively feeble power be applied for a much greater length of time. For example, if a line be drawn by a child in the earth with a light cane, and the cane be drawn five or six times successively along the same line, it will be found that a furrow has been made in the soil with scarcely any exertion by the child, that the strongest man could not make by a single effort with all his force. In the same way a lady, with a small light spade, may, by repeatedly digging over the same line, and taking out only a little earth at a time, succeed in doing, with her own hands, all the digging that can be required in a small garden, the soil of which, if it has been long in cultivation, can never be very hard, or very difficult to penetrate; and she will not only have the satisfaction of seeing the garden created, as it were, by the labour of her own hands, but she will find her health and spirits wonderfully improved by the exercise, and by the reviving smell of the fresh earth.

The first point to be attended to, in order to render the operation of digging less laborious, is to provide a suitable spade; that is, one which shall be as light as is consistent with strength, and which will penetrate the ground with the least possible trouble. For this purpose, the blade of what is called a lady's spade is made of not more than half the usual breadth, say not wider than five or six inches, and of smooth polished iron, and it is surmounted, at the part where it joins the handle, by a piece of iron rather broader than itself, which is called the tread, to serve as a rest for the foot of the operator while digging.

The handle is about the usual length, but quite smooth and sufficiently slender for the lady's hand to grasp, and it is made of willow, a close, smooth, and elastic wood, which is tough and tolerably strong, though much lighter than ash, the wood generally used for the handles to gardeners' spades. The lady should also be provided with clogs, the soles of which are not jointed, to put over her shoes; or if she should dislike these, and prefer strong shoes, she should be provided with what gardeners call a tramp, that is, a small plate of iron to go under the sole of the shoe, and which is fastened round the foot with

A Lady's Gauntlet of strong leather, invented by Miss Perry, near Hazlemere.

a leathern strap and buckle. She should also have a pair of stiff thick leather gloves, or gauntlets to protect her hands, not only from the handle of the spade, but from the stones, weeds, &c., which she may turn over with the earth, and which ought to be picked out and thrown into a small, light wheelbarrow, which may easily be moved from place to place.

A wheel-barrow is a lever of the second kind, in which the weight is carried between the operator, who is the moving power, and the fulcrum, which is represented by the lower part of the wheel. If it be so contrived that the wheel may roll on a plank, or on firm ground, a very slight power is sufficient to move the load contained in the barrow; particularly if the handles be long, curved, and thrown up as high as possible, in order to let the weight rest principally upon the wheel, without obliging the operator to bend forward. When, on the contrary, the handles are short and straight, the weight is thrown principally on the arms of the operator, and much more strength is required to move the load, besides the inconvenience of stooping.

All the necessary implements for digging being provided, the next thing to be considered is the easiest manner of performing the operation. The usual way is for the gardener to thrust his spade perpendicularly into the ground, and then using the handle as a lever, to draw it back so as to raise the whole mass of earth in front of the spade at once. This requires great strength; but by inserting the spade in a slanting direction, and throwing the body slightly forward at the same time, the mass of earth to be raised will not only be much less, but the body of the operator will be in a much more convenient position for raising and turning it; which may thus be done with perfect ease.

The time for digging should always be chosen, if possible, when the ground is tolerably dry; not only on account of the danger of taking cold by standing on the damp earth, but because the soil, when damp, adheres to the spade, and is much more difficult to work (as the gardeners call it,) than when it is dry. The ground in fields, &c. becomes very hard in dry weather; but this is never the case in a garden, the soil of which is well pulverized by the constant digging, forking, hoeing, and raking, it must undergo, to keep the garden tolerably neat. Every lady should be careful, when she has finished digging, to have her spade dipped in water, and then wiped dry: after which it should be hung up in some warm dry shed, or harness room, to keep it free from rust: as nothing lessens the labour of digging more

than having a perfectly smooth and polished spade. Should the
earth adhere to the spade while digging, dipping he blade in
water occasionally, will be found to facilitate the operation.

The purposes for which digging is applied in gardening are:
simple digging for loosening the soil in order to prepare it for a
crop; pointing; burying manure; exposing the soil to the action
of the weather; trenching; ridging; forming pits for planting
trees and shrubs, or for filling with choice soil for sowing seeds;
and taking up plants when they are to be removed.

In simple digging, as well as most of the other kinds, it is
customary to divide the bed to be dug, by a garden-line, into
two parts: a trench, or furrow as it is called, is then opened
across one of these divisions or half of the bed, the earth out
of which is thrown up into heap. The digging then commences
by turning over a breadth of soil into the furrow, thus made,
and so forming a new furrow to be filled up by the soil turned
over from the breadth beyond it; and this is continued till the
operator reaches the end of the first division, when the furrow
is to be filled with the earth taken from the first furrow of the
second division; after which the digging proceeds regularly as
before, till the operator reaches the last furrow, which is filled
with the ridge of earth thrown up when the first furrow was
made. As few ladies are strong enough to throw the earth from
the heap where it was laid from the first furrow to fill the last,
the best way is to put it into a small wheel-barrow, which may be
wheeled to the place required, and filled and emptied as often
as may be found convenient; or the ground may be divided into
narrower strips. It must also be observed, that as a spadeful

of earth taken up obliquely will seldom be found to loosen
the soil to a proper depth, a second or even a third should be
taken from the same place before the operator advances any
further along the line: or the whole of each furrow may be
made shallow, and then deepened by successive diggings before
proceeding to the next furrow.

It is obvious that the great art in this kind of digging is to
keep the furrows straight, and not to take up more earth in
one place than in another, so that the surface of the ground,
when finished, may be perfectly even. To keep the furrows
straight, the first ought to be marked out with the rod and line,
and every succeeding line should be frequently and carefully
examined. It is more difficult to keep these lines straight than
can be at first sight imagined: and in proportion as the furrow
is allowed to become crooked it will become narrower, and be
in danger of being choked up; or, if kept as wide as before, the
surface of the ground will be rendered uneven, and the last
furrow left without earth enough to fill it up. In digging each
furrow also, care must be taken to carry it quite up to the line
of demarcation; as, otherwise, what the gardeners call a baulk
or piece of firm land would be left there, and, of course, the
bed would neither look well, or would the object for which it
was dug be fully attained. Great care must also be taken to keep
the surface of the bed even, and this it is extremely difficult
for a novice to do. It is, indeed, very provoking, after watching
the ease with which a gardener digs a bed, and looking at the
perfectly smooth and even surface that he leaves, to find how
hard it is to imitate him; and yet it is essentially necessary to

be done, for if there are any irregularities in the surface, the hollow places will collect the moisture, and the plants in them will grown vigorously, while those in the raised places will be speedily dried by the sun and wind, and will look poor and withered. Practice is certainly required to render digging easy, but, as the principle points of keeping the furrows straight, and the surface even, depend on skill more than strength, the art of digging well may be acquired by any one who thinks it worth while to take the trouble. Very little strength will, indeed, be necessary, if the rule of thrusting in the spade obliquely, and aiding it by the momentum of the body, be always attended to.

Pointing, as it is called by gardeners, is in fact shallow digging, and it consists in merely turning over the ground to the depth of two or three inches. In spring, or in the beginning of summer, when the sun had only warmed the soil to the depth of a few inches, and when the seeds to be sown (as of annual flowers for example) are wanted to germinate as quickly as possible, pointing is preferable to digging; because the latter operation would bury the warm soil, and bring that up to the surface which is still as cold as in winter. Pointing is also used in stirring the ground among trees and other plants, in order that the spade may not go so deeply into the ground as to injure their roots.

Burying manure
There are two ways of digging the ground for the purpose of burying manure: according to the first method, the manure

is spread evenly over the whole bed, and then the gardener
proceeds to dig as though the manure were in fact a portion of
the surface of the soil; and according to the second method, the
manure having been first brought to the spot and thrown into
a heap, is deposited, a small portion at a time, at the bottom
of each furrow as it is formed, and the earth from the next
furrow thrown over it. In both cases, the manure should be
buried as speedily as possible; as if left long exposed in small
quantities to the air in hot dry weather, it loses a great part of
its nutritious qualities by evaporation.

Digging for the purpose of exposing the soil to the action
of the weather, trenching, and ridging on a large scale, are
operations too laborious to be performed by any one but a
gardener's labourer. To be done well, the earth in all these cases
should be removed in large spadefuls at a time, and turned over
without breaking; on which account these operations are best
performed in moist weather, when the earth is in an adhesive
state. Ridging on a small scale may be useful in a flower garden,
when the soil is much infested with insects, or where there are
many weeds. It is performed by opening a trench, and throwing
up the earth out of it in the form of a ridge in the same manner.
The whole garden is thus thrown into a series of ridges and
trenches, which should be suffered to remain all the winter, and
be levelled in spring. It is obvious that this mode of ameliorating
the soil can only be practised where the garden is not likely to
be visited during the winter, as it destroys all beauty, and has a
peculiarly desolate and forlorn appearance. It is thus a remedy
only to be resorted to in extreme cases; but fortunately there

are very few flower gardens in which the soil is in so bad a state as to require it.

The other kinds of digging are to form pits for receiving plants, or for filling with choice soil, and to remove plants. In the first case, a hole of sufficient size to receive the plant is dug, and the earth thrown up beside it, to be filled in round the roots of the plant; and in the second case, the common garden earth is thrown out of a pit a foot or eighteen inches deep, and about the same in diameter, and its place supplied by peat, or whatever other kind of earth may be required. In removing a young tree or shrub, the ground is generally first dug out on one side, so as to form a small trench, and then the spade is driven perpendicularly into the ground, below the depth to which the roots descent, and the whole mass is raised like a spadeful of earth. Small plants are raised by the spade at once without making any trench; and large trees require all the skill of a professed gardener.

Forking

A broad-pronged garden fork may be defined as an implement consisting of a number of small sharply pointed spades, united by a shoulder or hilt, to which is fixed the handle; and forking differs from digging, principally in its being used merely to stir the soil, and not to turn it over. In shrubberies, and among perennial herbaceous plants, which are not to be taken up and replanted, forking is very useful, as it loosens the hard dry surface of the soil, and admits the warm air and rain to the roots of the plants. This is very necessary, as the earth is a bad conductor of heat; and where the surface of the soil is become so hard as to exclude the air from the roots of the plants, the ground in which they grown will be nearly as cold in summer as in winter. Besides, when the surface of the ground is hard, the rain, instead of soaking gradually into it, runs off, or evaporates, without being of any service to the roots. The operation of forking consists merely in thrusting the fork a little way into the ground by the application of the foot to the hilt, and then pulling back the handle as in digging, so as to loosen the earth without raising it. The ground may thus be roughly pulverized to a considerable depth, without dividing the roots of the plants; which would have bee inevitable if the operator had used a spade.

Hoeing

There are several different kinds of hoes which are used for getting up weeds, for loosening the soil, for drawing it up round the stems of growing plants, and for making a shallow furrow or drill for sowing seeds. The different kinds all belong to two great divisions: viz. the draw hoe and the thrust hoe, and may be seen at any ironmonger's shop. Either kind may be used for destroying weeds; as the weeds may either be loosened and lifted out of the soil by the thrust hoe, or torn out of it by the draw hoe. Both kinds may also be used for pulverizing the soil, or a third kind with two prongs may be substituted. In all these operations, the thrust hoe is best adapted for a lady's use, as requiring the least exertion of strength, and being most easily managed; but the draw hoe is best adapted for making a drill or furrow for the reception of seeds, and also for the last and most

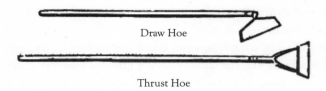

Draw Hoe

Thrust Hoe

important use of hoeing, viz. the drawing up of the earth round the stems of growing plants.

The operation of hoeing up, though very commonly practised is only suitable to some kind of plants, and it is intended to afford additional nourishment to those which have tap-roots, by inducing them to throw out more lateral fibres.

The plants which will bear to be hoed or earthed up, are those that throw out fibrous roots above the vital knot, like the cabbage tribe, &c.; or that are annuals with long bushy stems, and very weak and slender roots like the pea. Ligneous plants should never be earthed up to avoid injuring the vital knot, which forms the point of separation between the main root and the stem, and which gardeners call the collar, crown, neck or collet. This part in trees and shrubs should never be buried; as if it be injured by moisture so as to cause it to rot, or if it be wounded in any way, the plant will die. A deciduous tree may be cut down close above the collar, and it will throw up fresh shoots, or the roots may all be cut off close below the collar, and if that part be uninjured fresh roots will form; but if a tree be cut though at this vital part it never can recover.

A trowel is another instrument used in stirring the soil,

but of course it can only be employed in boxes of earth in balconies, &c.

Raking is useful in smoothing the soil after digging, and in collecting weeds, stones, &c., and dragging them to one side, where they may be easily removed. An iron-toothed rake is generally used for the ground, and a wooden one for collecting grass after mowing. When it is wished that the teeth of the rake should enter the ground, the handle should be held low; but if the object is the collection of weed, &c., the handle should be held high. Dry weather is essential to raking the ground, as the principle use of the operation is to break the clods left by the spade; but raking together grass or weeds may be performed in wet weather.

The degree of strength required for raking depends partly upon the breadth of the head of the rake, and the number of its teeth, but principally upon the manner of holding it. If the rake be held low, it is obvious that greater strength will be required to drag it through the ground than if it is held high, in which case very little labour will be required to overcome the resistance it will meet with.

Ixia

Griffinia, Phycella

CHAPTER II

MANURING THE SOIL AND
MAKING HOT-BEDS

MOST persons imagine that manure is all that is wanted to make a garden fruitful; and thus, if the fruit-trees do not bear, and the flowers and vegetables do not thrive, manure is considered to be the universal panacea. Now, the fact is, that so far from this being the case, most small gardens have been manured a great deal too much; and in many, the surface soil, instead of consisting of rich friable mould, only presents a soft black shining substance, which is the humic acid from manure saturated with stagnant water. No appearance is more common in the gardens of street-houses than this, from these gardens being originally ill drained, and yet continually watered; and from their possessors loading them with manure, in the hope of rendering them fertile.

As it is known to chemists that it is principally the humic acid, and carbonic acid gas, contained in manure, which make that substance nourishing to plants; and as these acids must be dissolved in water before the roots can take them up, it may seem strange that any solution of them in water, however strong it may be, should be injurious to vegetation. The fact is, however, that it is the great quantity of food contained in the water that renders it unwholesome. When the roots of a plant and their little sponge-like terminations, are examined in a powerful microscope, it will be clearly seen that no thick substance can pass through them. Thus water loaded with gross coarse matter, as it is when saturated with humic acid, must be more than the poor spongioles can swallow; and yet, as they are truly spongelike, their nature prompts them, whenever they find moisture, to attempt to take it up, without having the power of discriminating between what is good for them, and what will be injurious. The spongioles thus imbibe the saturated liquid; and, loaded with this improper food, the fibrous roots, like an overgorged snake, become distended, the fine epidermis that covers them is torn asunder, their power of capillary attraction is gone, and they can neither force the food they have taken up, into the main roots, nor reject the excrementitious matter sent down to them from the leaves, after the elaboration of the sap. In this state of things, from the usual circulation of the fluids being impeded, it is not surprising that the plant should droop, that its leaves should turn yellow, that its flowers should not expand, that its fruit should shrivel and drop off prematurely, and that in the end it should die; as, in fact, it may be said to expire of apoplexy, brought on by indigestion.

All soil, to be in a fit state for growing plants, should be sufficiently loose and dry to allow of passing through it intermixed with air; as water, when in this state, is never more than slightly impregnated with the nutritious juices of the manure through which it has passed. The spongioles are thus not supplied with more food at a time than they can properly take up and digest, and a healthy circulation of the fluids is kept up through the whole plant. But, what, it may be asked, is to be done with a garden, the soil of which has become black and slimy like half-rotten peat? The quickest remedy is covering it with lime, as that combines readily with the humic acid, and reduces it to a state of comparative dryness: or, if the sub-soil be good, the ground may be trenched, and the surface-soil buried two spits deep; but in both cases it will be necessary thoroughly to drain the garden to prevent a recurrence of the evil.

All the different kinds of soil found on level ground, consist of two parts, which are called the surface-soil and the sub-soil; and as the sub-soil always consists of one of the three primitive earths, so do these earths always enter, more or less, into the composition of every kind of surface-soil. The primitive earths are – silex, (which includes sand and gravel,) clay, and lime, which includes also chalk; and most sub-soils consist of a solid bed or rock of one or other of these materials, probably in nearly the same state as it was left by the deluge.

The surface-soils, on the contrary, are of comparatively recent date; and they have been slowly formed by the gradual crumbling of the sub-soil, and its intermixture with decayed animal and vegetable matter, and with other soils which may have been accidentally washed down upon, or purposely brought to it. In fields, and uncultivated places, the surface-soil is almost as hard, and as course in its texture, as the sub-soil on which it rests; but in gardens which have been long in cultivation, the surface-soil becomes so thoroughly pulverized by frequent diggings, and so mixed with the manure and decayed vegetables which have been added to it from time to time, that it is changed into the soft, light, fine, powdery substance, called garden-mould. If the sub-soil be naturally porous or well drained, this mould, however rich it may be made by the addition of decayed vegetable matter or animal manure, will always continue friable; and as long as it does so, it will be fit for the growth of plants: but if no vent be allowed for the escape of the water, and it be continually enriched with manure, it will be changed in time into the black slimy substance hat has been already described.

Surface-soil is called peat-earth when it is composed of decayed vegetable matter, which has become partially decayed by time and immersion in water, but which is not thoroughly decomposed. As this kind of earth cannot exist without abundance of stagnant moisture, it is almost always found on a clayey sub-soil, which prevents the water which falls upon it from escaping. Peat-earth has a spongy elastic feeling when trodden upon, arising from the quantity of water that it holds, and it can only be rendered fit for cultivation by draining; or depriving it in some other manner of its superabundant moisture. In its elastic state it is what is called in Scotland a moss, and in England a peat-bog. Should the water, instead of being afforded a vent by drainage, be suffered to accumulate for many years, till it completely liquefies the peat, the soil becomes what is called a morass, or quagmire; and it can no longer be trodden on, as it will engulf any substance resting upon it. A still further accumulation of water will, in the course of years, cause the bog to burst its bounds, and overflow the surrounding country; as the Solway-moss did many years ago, as bogs in Ireland have done frequently. An excess of vegetable matter on a sandy or gravelly sub-soil, differs from the common black-peat in retaining less water; and in being mixed with a portion of the primitive earth, which, from its loose texture, becomes easily detached from the sub-soil and mixes with the surface-soil; which, when in this state, is called heath mould.

The most productive soils are those in which several ingredients are combined in proper proportions; and if any one of the primitive earths preponderates, the soil becomes comparatively unfertile. Thus the best soil for gardening purposes is generally allowed to be a calcareous loam on a chalky sub-soil; and this sort of soil is composed of nearly equal parts of lime, sand, and clay, enriched by depositions of decayed animal and vegetable matter. The next best soil is a sandy loam, composed of clay and sand, enriched by decayed animal and vegetable substances, and resting on a sandy or gravelly sub-soil. The worst soils are black peat, and loose sand. A poor sandy soil is necessarily a nearly barren one; because it will not retain either water, or the nutritious juices from manure, long enough to afford nourishment to the plants grown upon it; and it is obvious that a soil of this kind can only be rendered fertile by mixing it with clay, which would change it into a sandy loam.

A stiff clay is unfertile from its attracting moisture and retaining it round the roots of the plants till they become swollen and unhealthy. It also retards the decomposition of manure, and obstructs the progress of the roots, which waste their strength in the efforts they make to penetrate, or twine round, its adhesive clods. Soils of this description are improved by a mixture of sand, gravel, road grit, or any substance which tends to separate the particles of the clay, and to render it light and friable.

Chalky soils succeed better unmixed, than any of the other kinds; but chalk being a carbonate of lime, can hardly be called a primitive soil. The chalk, however, from its whiteness, is colder than any other soil; as it does not absorb, but reflects back the rays of the sun. Rain also penetrates into it very slowly, and not to any great depth. Chalk mixed with sand forms a kind of calcareous loam admirably adapted for growing vegetables; and chalky soils are peculiarly susceptible of improvement from manure.

Black peat, though it abounds in vegetable matter, is not, in its natural state, favourable for the growth of plants; as it abounds in tannin, which prevents the decomposition of the vegetable fibre. Thus peat bogs can only be rendered fertile by the addition of lime, or some other material, which will absorb or neutralise the tannin with which they are imbued, and thus permit the vegetable substances which they contain, to decompose, so as to form nutritive matter for the growing plants. This, however, is only the case with the black peat, for heath mould or sandy peat, which is what is generally called peat earth in gardens, is very useful, even in its natural state, for the growth of all hair-rooted plants, such as the Cape Heaths; the Rhodeodendrons, and other American plants; and all the Australian shrubs. The reason of this difference is, that the mixture of sand with the peat prevents its retention of water; and it is only the retention of water around the vegetable fibre which prevents its decomposition. Thus where natural heath mould cannot be procured, mixing the black peat with fine white sand has the effect of rendering it suitable for the growth of hair-rooted plants.

Manures

The kinds of manure generally used in gardens are horse or cow dung, and decayed vegetable matters; the manure in both cases being suffered to lie in a heap to rot before it is spread on the ground, in order that its component parts may be decomposed by fermentation, and thus brought into a fit state to afford food to the plants. Old hot-beds or mushroom beds are thus well adapted for manuring a garden; and when fresh stable-dung is employed for that purpose, it is generally thrown into a heap, and turned over several times till the fermentation has abated, before it is dug into the ground. As, however, a great quantity of the manure is dissolved and washed away by the rain which falls upon the heap, while it is undergoing the process of fermentation, and as it seems a great pity that so much of the nutritious properties of the manure should be lost, a quantity of earth should always be laid round the dung-hill to imbibe the liquid that runs from it, and this earth will be found very nearly as valuable for manuring the beds of a garden, as the manure itself.

The properties of horse and cow dung, considered as manures, vary exceedingly; the former abounding in nitrogen, in which the latter is nearly deficient. All manures abounding in nitrogen are called by gardeners hot; because the gases they evolve, if too strong, blacken the plants as though they had been exposed to the action of fire; and on the contrary, all the manures which do not evolve gases producing this effect, and termed by the gardeners cold.

The modes of applying manure differ according to the difference of the soils. For sandy loams, thoroughly rotten dung,

either from an old hot-bed, or from a dung-hill sufficiently
decayed to be cut easily with the spade, should be laid on the
surface of the soil, and dug in. In very poor sandy soils, rotten
manure, or earth saturated with liquid manure from a dung-
hill, should be laid on the surface of the soil, and not dug in:
the manure being covered, if hot dry weather be expected,
with leaves, straw, or the branches of trees cut off in pruning,
or occasionally sprinkled with water. Soils consisting of poor,
and partly loose sand, are frequently improved in the South of
France and Italy, but sowing them with the seeds of the common
white lupine, and then, when the plants have come up and are
grown about a foot high, ploughing or digging them into the soil.
The green succulent stems of the lupines, when thus buried in
the soil, supply it with moisture during the progress of their
decay; and thus nourishment is afforded to the corn, which is
immediately afterwards sown upon the soil for a crop.

Clayey soils should have unfermented manure mixed with
undecayed straw laid in the bottom off the furrow made in
digging; that the process of fermentation, and the remains of
the straw may operate in keeping the particles of the soil open,
or, in other words, in preventing their too close adhesion. Lime
as a manure can very seldom be employed advantageously in
gardens and pleasure grounds; only indeed where there is a
superabundance of humic acid, as described previously. When
applied to grass, as it frequently is, it has been found by repeated
experiments to sink down through the soil, without mixing
with it, and to form a distinct stratum an inch or two below the
surface of the soil. This may be seen in several places where the

ground has been cut through for railroads; particularly in the Midland counties railroad, near Leicester, where the lime which has been applied to the grass land, forms a narrow white line, very conspicuous from the red sandstone of the district. Lime should, therefore, be always well mixed with the soil when used as a manure; and when burnt, it should be used alone, as it will destroy and waste all the animal manure applied with it. As carbonate of lime, or chalk, however, (in which state only it can properly be called a soil,) animal manure may be applied to it with great advantage, and it will retain its efficacy longer than with any other soil. Rotten manure may be dug into chalk, with the certainty that it will be preserved from further decay for a very long time, and that every shower will work a small portion of its fertilizing juices out of it, and carry them into the soil, where they will be thus presented to the plants in the best possible state for affording wholesome food.

Peat bogs may be improved by the addition of quick-lime as a manure, which will absorb the superabundant moisture which they contain, and will thus permit their vegetable fibre to decompose. Peat, when saturated with water, abounds in tannin; and this substance preserves both vegetable and animal matter from decomposition. Thus, as no growing plant can absorb nutriment from vegetable matter, unless it be first thoroughly decomposed, peat, though abounding in the elements necessary for the food of pants, can afford them no nourishment till it has been deprived of its superfluous moisture. Heath mould does not require any substance to absorb its moistures, as the sand with which is is mixed answers that purpose; and from the quantity of vegetable matter that it contains naturally, it does not require any manure, more than what is furnished by the decaying leaves of the pants grown in it.

Nearly the same rules apply to decaying leaves and other substances used as manure, as to stable-dung. They may be buried in an undecayed state in clayey soil, when the object is to separate the adhesive particles of the clay by the process of fermentation; but their component parts should be separated by fermentation before they are applied as a manure to growing plants. Vegetable mould (that is, leaves thoroughly decayed and mixed with a little rich loam,) is admirably adapted for manuring the finer kinds of flowers, and plants in pots. There are many other kinds of manure used in gardens occasionally; such as dung of pigs, rabbits and poultry, grass mown from lawns, parings of leather, horn shavings, bones, the sweeping of streets, the emptying of privies, cess-pools, and sewers, the clipping of hedges and pruning of trees, weeds, the refuse of vegetables, pea-halm, &c. All these should be fermented and applied in the same manner as the common kinds of manure.

The following is a summary of the general rules to be observed in manuring and improving soils:–

Never to use animal manure and quick-lime together, as the one will destroy the other.

To use lime as a manure only in very moist peaty soils, or in soils which have been injured by want of drainage, and a superabundance of manure.

To take care that lime, when applied, is mixed intimately

with the soil, and not laid on the surface to be washed in by the rain.

To remember that rotten manure is considered to give solidity; and that unfermented manure, buried in trenching, has a tendency to lighten the soil.

To dilute liquid manure from a dung-hill with water, before applying it to growing plants; as otherwise, from the quantity of amonia that it contains it will be apt to burn them.

To remember that the manure of cows and all animals that chew the cud, is cold and suited to a light soil; and that the manure of horses, pigs, and poultry is hot and suited to a firm soil: also that all manure, when new, may be considered as hot, from the heat that will be engendered during the process of fermentiation; and that when well rotten, it becomes cold in its nature, and should be treated accordingly.

To remember that all mixed soils are more fertile than soils consisting only of one of three primitive earths, viz., lime, sand, or clay; and never to forget that too much manure is quite as injurious to plants as too little.

Formation of hot beds

Though nearly all the kinds of manure which have been enumerated may be used occasionally for hot-beds, the only materials in common use in gardens are stable manure, dead leaves, and tan. The first of these, which is by far the most general, consists partly of horse-dung, and partly of what gardeners call long litter, that it, straw moistened and discoloured, but not decayed. The manure is generally in this state when it is purchased, or taken from the stable, for the purpose of making a hot-bed.

The necessary quantity of manure is procured, at the rate of one cart load, or from twelve to fifteen large wheel-barrowfuls, to every light, (as the gardeners call the sashes of the frames,) each light being about three feet wide; and this manure is laid in a heap to ferment. In about a week the manure should be turned over with a dung-fork, and well shaken together; this operation being repeated two or three, or more times, at intervals of two or three days, till the whole mass is become of one colour, and the straws are sufficiently decomposed to be torn to pieces with the fork.

The size of the hot-bed must depend principally on the size of the frame which is to cover it; observing that the bed must be from six inches to a foot wider than the frame every way. The manure must then be spread in layers, each layer being beaten down with the back of the fork, till the bed is about three feet and a half high. The surface of the ground on which the hot-bed is built, is generally raised about six inches above the general surface of the garden; and it is advisable to lay some earth round the bottom of the bed, nearly a foot wide, that it may receive the juices of the manure that will drain from the bed. As soon as the bed is made, the frame is put on and the sashes kept quite close, till a steam appears upon the glass, when the bed is considered in a fit state to be covered three or four inches deep with mould; observing, if the bed has settled unequally, to level the surface of the manure before covering it with earth. The seeds to be raised may either be sown in this earth, or in posts to be plunged in it.

The proper average heat for a hot-bed intended to raise flower seeds, or to grow cucumbers, is 60°: but melons require a heat of 65° to grow in, and 75° to ripen their fruit. This heat should be taken in a morning, and does not include that of the sun in the middle of the day. When the heat of the bed becomes so great as to be in danger of injuring the plants, the obvious remedy is to give air by raising the glasses; and if this be not sufficient, the general heat of the bed must be lowered by making excavations in the dung from the sides, so as to reach nearly the middle of the bed, and filling up these excavations with cold dung which has already undergone fermentation, or with leaves, turf, or any other similar material which will receive heat, but not increase it. When the heat of the bed falls down to 48° or lower, it should be raised, by applying on the outside fresh coatings of dung, grass, or leaves, which are called linings.

When hot-beds are made of spent tanner's bark or decayed leaves, a kind of box or pit must be formed of bricks or boards, or even of layers of turf, or clay, and the tan of leaves filled in so as to make a bed. Where neatness is an object, this kind of bed is preferable to any other; but a common hot-bed of stable manure may be made to look neat by thatching the outside with straw, or covering it with bast mats, pegged down to keep them close to the bed.

Helleborus, Trollius, Isopyrum, Coptis, Eranthus

CHAPTER III

SOWING SEEDS, PLANTING BULBS AND TUBERS, TRANSPLANTING AND WATERING

Sowing Seeds

The principal points to be attended to in sowing seeds are, first, to prepare the ground so that the young and tender roots thrown out by the seeds may easily penetrate into it; secondly, to fix the seeds firmly in the soil; thirdly, to cover them, so as to exclude the light, which impedes vegetation, and to preserve a sufficiency of moisture round them to encourage it; and, fourthly, not be bury them so deeply as either to deprive them of the beneficial influence of the air, or to throw any unnecessary impediments in the way of their ascending shoots.

The preparation of the soil has been already described in the chapter on digging, and the reasons why it is necessary have been there given; but why seeds should be firmly imbedded in it, seems to require explanation. It is well known that gardeners, before they either sow a bed in the kitchen-garden, or a patch of flower-seeds in the flower-garden, generally "firm the ground," as they call it, by beating it well with the back of the spade, or pressing it with the saucer of a flower-pot; and there can be no doubt that this is done in order that the seeds may be firmly imbedded in the soil. When lawns are sown with grass-seeds also, the seeds are frequently rolled in, evidently for the same purpose. The only question, therefore, is, why is this necessary? and the answer appears to be, that a degree of permanence and stability is essential to enable nature to accommodate the plant to the situation in which it is placed. When there is this degree of permanence and stability, it is astonishing to observe the efforts that plants will make to provide for their wants; but without it, seeds will not even vegetate. Thus we often see large trees springing from crevices in apparently bare rocks; while not even a blade of grass will grown among the moving sands of a desert.

The reasons for the second and third points of covering the seeds, and yet not covering them too deeply, appear more obvious; and yet they also require a little explanation. The seeds are covered to keep them in darkness, and to retain round them a proper quantity of moisture; not only to make them swell and begin to vegetate, but to enable the roots to perform their proper functions; since, if exposed to the air, they would become dry and withered, and lose the power of contracting ad dilating, which is essential to enable them to imbibe and digest their food.

Burying the seeds too deeply is obviously injurious in impeding the progress of the young shoot to the light; and in placing it in an unnatural position. When a seed vegetates too far below the surface, a part of the stem of the plant must be buried; and this part not being intended to remain underground, is not protected from the dangers it is likely to meet with there. It is thus peculiarly liable to be assailed by slugs and all kinds of insects, and to become rotten by damp, or withered by heat. It is also very possibly to bury a seed so deeply as to prevent it from vegetating at all. The ground has more of both warmth and moisture near the surface than at a great depth, as it is warmed by the rays of the sun, and moistened by the rain; but besides this, seeds will not vegetate, even when they are amply supplied with heat and moisture, if they are excluded from the influence of the air. Every ripe seed in a dry state is a concentration of carbon, which, when dissolved by moisture, and its particles set in motion by heat, is in a fit state to combine with oxygen in the atmosphere, and thus to form the carbonic acid gas which is the nourishment of the expanding plant. For this reason, seeds and newly sprung-up plants do not want to be supplied with manure, and air is much more essential to them: they have enough carbon in their cotyledons, or in the albumen contained in the seed, and they only want oxygen to combine with it, to enable them to develop their other leaves; and this is the reason why young plants, raised on ta hot-bed, are always given air, or they become yellow and withered. Light absorbs the oxygen from plants, and occasions a deposition of the carbon. Thus seeds and seedlings do not require much light; it is indeed injurious to them, as it undoes in some degree what the air has been doing for them: but young plants, when they have expanded two or three pairs of leaves, and when the stock of carbon contained in their cotyledons, or in their seeds, is exhausted, require light to enable them to elaborate their sap, without which the process of vegetation could not go on.

Abundance of light also is favourable to the development of flowers and the ripening of seeds; as it aids the concentration of carbon, which they require to make them fertile. The curious fact that seeds, though abundantly supplied with warmth and moisture, will not vegetate without the assistance of the air, was lately verified in Italy; where the Po, having overflowed its banks near Mantua, deposited a great quantity of mud on some meadows; and from this mud sprang up a plentiful crop of black poplars, no doubt from seeds that had fallen into the river from a row of trees of that kind, which had formerly grown on its banks, but which had been cut down many years previously. Another instance occurred in the case of some raspberry seeds found in the body of an ancient Briton discovered in a tumulus in Dorsetshire. Some of these seeds were sown in the London Horticultural Society's Garden at Turnham Green, where they vegetated, and the plants produced form them are still (1840) growing. Numerous other nearly similar instances will be found in *Hooker's Botanical Miscellany, Lindley's theory of Horticulture, Jesse's Gleanings,* and numerous other works. Steeping seeds in oxalic acid, &c. to make them vegetate, is efficacious; as there is a speedier combination between the carbon in the seeds, and the oxygen in the acid, than can be effected by the ordinary agency of the air in parting with its oxygen to them.

Planting bulbs and tubers

Planting bulbs and tubers bears considerable analogy to sowing seeds. The bulb or tuber may indeed be considered as only a seed of larger growth, since it requires the combined influence of air, warmth, and moisture to make it vegetate, and then it throws out a stem, leaves, and roots like a seed. There is, however, one important difference between them; the seed expends its accumulated stock of carbon in giving birth to the root, stem,

Tulipa

and leaves, after which it withers away and disappears; while the bulb or tuber continues to exist during the whole life of the plant, and appears to contain a reservoir of carbon, which it only parts with slowly, and as circumstances may require. Though bulbs and tubers have here been mentioned as almost synonymous, modern botanists make several distinctions between them. The tunicated bulbs, such as those of the hyacinth and the onion, and the squamose bulbs, such as those of the lily, they consider to be underground buds; while tubers, such as those of the dahlia, and the potato, and solid bulbs or corms, such as those of the crocus, they regard as underground stems.

These distinctions, however, though they may be interesting to the botanist and vegetable physiologist, are of little or no use in practice; the practical gardener treating bulbs and tubers exactly alike, and planting them as he would sow a seed: that is to say, he fixes them firmly in the ground, and covers them, but not so deeply as to exclude the air. In preparing a bed for hyacinths or other tunicated bulbs, it is necessary to pulverize the soil to a much greater depth than for ordinary seeds; as the true roots of the hyacinth descend perpendicularly to a considerable depth, as may be seen when these plants are grown in glasses. The very circumstance of growing hyacinths in glasses, where they vegetate and send down their roots exposed to the full influence of the light, appears contrary to the usual effects of light on vegetation; and indeed the plants are said generally to thrive best, when the glasses are kept in the dark till the roots are half grown. However this may be, it is quite certain that hyacinths in glasses should never be kept in darkness after their leaves have begun to expand; as if there be not abundance of light to occasion rapid evaporation from the leaves, the plants will soon become surcharged with moisture from the quantity constantly supplied to their roots, and the leaves will turn yellow, and look flaccid, and unhealthy, while the flowers will be stunted, or will fall off without expanding.

Transplanting

The points to be attended to in transplanting, are – care in taking up, to avoid injuring the spongioles of the roots; planting firmly, to enable the plant to take a secure hold of the soil; shading, to prevent the evaporation from the leaves from being greater than the plant in its enfeebled state can support; and watering, that it may be abundantly supplied with food in its new abode. The first point is to avoid injuring the roots, and it is only necessary to consider the construction and uses of these most important organs to perceive how impossible it is for the plant to thrive, unless they are in a perfectly healthy state.

Roots generally consist of two parts; the main roots, which are intended to act as grappling irons to enable the plants to take a firm hold of the ground, and the fibrous roots, which are intended to supply the plant with nourishment. These fibrous roots are most liable to receive injury from transplanting, as they are covered with a very fine cellular integument, so delicate in its texture as to be very easily bruised; and they each terminate in a number of small pores of extraordinary delicacy and susceptibility, which act as little sponges to imbibe moisture for the use of the plant. It is well known that these spongioles are the only means which the plant possesses of imbibing food, and that if they should be all cut off, the plant must provide itself with others, or perish for want of nourishment. These spongioles are exactly of the nature of a sponge; they expand at the approach of moisture, and when surcharged with it, they contract, and thus force it into the fibrous roots, the cellular integument of which dilates to receive it; hence the moisture is forced, (by capillary attraction, as it is supposed,) into the main roots, and thence into the stem and branches of the plant; circulating like the blood, and, after it has been elaborated and turned into sap in the leaves, as the blood is changed in its nature in the lungs, dispensing nourishment to every part as it goes along.

The roots have no pores but those forming the spongioles; and only the fibrous roots appear to possess the power of alternate dilation and contraction, which power evidently depends on their cellular tissue being in an entire and healthy state. Thus, it is quite evident that if the spongiole of any fibril be crushed, or even the cellular tissue injured, it can no longer act as a mouth and throat to convey food to the plant. When this is the case, the injured part should be instantly removed; as its elasticity can never be restored, and it is much better for the plant to be forced to throw out a new fibril, than to be obliged to carry on its circulation weakly and imperfectly with a diseased one. Whenever a plant is taken up for transplanting, its roots should therefore be carefully examined, and all their injured parts cut off, before it is replaced in the ground. Deciduous plants, and particularly trees and shrubs, are generally transplanted when they are without their leaves; because at that season they are in no danger of suffering from the effects of evaporation.

Shading is necessary after transplanting any plant that retains its leaves; as the evaporation from the leaves, if exposed to the full action of the light, would be greater than the plant could support with a diminished number of spongioles. If it were possible to transplant without injuring the fibrils, and if the plant were immediately supplied with plenty of water, shading would not be required; and, indeed, when plants are turned out of a pot into the open garden without breaking the ball of earth round their roots, they are never shaded. The reason for this is, that as long as a plant remains where it was first sown, and under favourable circumstances, the evaporation from its leaves is exactly adapted to its powers of absorbing moisture; it is therefore evident, that if, by any chance, the number of its mouths be diminished, the evaporation from its leaves should be checked also, till the means of supplying a more abundant evaporation are restored.

The use of watering a transplanted plant, is as obvious as that of shading. It is simply to supply the spongioles with an abundance of food, that the increased quantity imbibed by each, may, in some degree, supply their diminished number.

All plants will not bear transplanting, and those that have tap-roots, such as the carrot, are peculiarly unfitted for it. When plants having tap-roots are transplanted, it should be into very light soil, and what is called a puddle should be made to receive them. To do this, a hole or pit should be formed, deeper than the root of the plant, and into this pit water should be poured and earth thrown in it and stirred, so as it half-fill it with mud. The tap-rooted plant should then be plunged into the mud,

Hyacinthus

shaking it a little so as to let the mud penetrate among its fibrous roots, and the pit should be then filled in with light soil. The plant must afterwards be shaded longer than is usual with other plants; and when water is given, it should be poured down nearer the to the main root than in other cases, as the lateral fibrous roots never spread far from it. Plants with spreading roots, when transplanted, should have the pit intended to receive them, made shallow, but very wide in its diameter; so that the roots may be spread out in it to their fullest extent, except those that appear at all bruised or injured, which, as before directed, should be cut off with a sharp knife.

It is a general rule, in transplanting, never to bury the collar of a plant; though this rule has some exceptions in the case of annuals. Some of these, such as balsams, send out roots from the stem above the collar; and these plants are always very much improved by transplanting. Others, the fibrous roots of which are long and descending, such as hyacinths, bear transplanting very ill, and when it is absolutely necessary to remove them, it should be done with an instrument called a transplanter; which may be purchased in any ironmonger's shop, and the use of which is to take up a sufficient quantity of earth with the plant to remove it without disturbing the roots.

The uses of transplanting are various. When seeds are sown, and the young plants from them begin to make their appearance, they will generally be found to be much too thick; and they will require thinning, either by drawing some of them out and throwing them away, or by removing them to another bed by transplanting. This, in the case of annuals, is called by

the gardeners pricking out. The young plants are taken up with
a small trowel, and replaced in a hole made for them, and the
earth pressed round them, with the same trowel: the only care
necessary, being to make them firm at the root, and yet to avoid
injuring the tender spongioles. Gardeners do this with a dibber,
which they hold in the right hand, and after putting in the young
plant with the left hand, they press the earth round it with the
dibber in a manner that I never could manage to imitate. I have
found the trowel, however, do equally well, though it takes up
rather more time.

Another use of transplanting is to remove trees and shrubs
from the nursery to where they are permanently to remain.
To enable this to be done with safety, the trees and shrubs in
commercial nurseries are prepared by being always removed
every year, or every other year, whether they are sold or not. The
effect of these frequent removals is to keep the roots short, and
yet provided with numerous spongioles; for as they are always
pruned, or as the gardeners call it, "cut in," on every removal,
and as the effect of pruning is to induce the roots pruned to send
out two short fibrous roots armed with spongioles, in the place
of every one cut off, the roots, though confined to a small space,
become abundant. The reverse of this is the case, when plants
are left in a natural state. It has been found, from experience,
that plants imbibe more food that they absolutely require as
nourishment from the soil, and that they eject part of it; also that
their roots will not re-imbibe this excrementitious matter, but are
continually in search of fresh soil. To provide for this the fibrous
roots are possessed of an extraordinary power of elongating

themselves at their extremities; and thus the roots of even a small plant, left to nature, will be found to extend to a great distance on every side. It is obvious that this elongation of the roots must greatly increase the difficulties attending transplanting. Where the roots extend to a distance from the trees, a greater extent of ground has to be disturbed, both to take up the plant, and to make a pit for replanting it; the risk of injuring the fibrous roots is increased; and, as nearly all the spongioles will require to be cut off from the great length of the roots, and consequent great difficulty which will attend taking them up entire, the plant will be nearly famished before new spongioles can be formed to supply it with food. All these dangers are avoided by the nursery system of transplanting; while the inconvenience of confining the roots to so small a space is obviated, by placing the plant, every time it is transplanted, in fresh soil.

It is customary, when trees or shrubs are transplanted to the places where they are permanently to remain, either to make a puddle for them, or to fix them, as it is called, with water; the object, in both cases, being to supply the pant with abundance of food in its new situation. Care is taken, also, to make the roots firm in the soil, and to let the earth penetrate through all their interstices. To attain these ends, one gardener generally holds the tree and gently shakes it, while another is shovelling in the earth among its roots: but this mode has the disadvantage of sometimes occasioning the roots to become matted. When the tree is to be fixed with water, after a little earth has been shovelled in over the roots, water is applied by pouring it from a watering-pot, held as high as a man can raise it; the watering-pot used being large, and with a wide spout, the rose of which must be taken off. More earth is then shovelled in, and water applied again. This mode of planting has the great advantage of rendering the tree firm, without staking, or treading the earth down round it, as is usually done. Other gardeners spread the roots out carefully at the bottom of the hole or pit made to receive them, and then fill in the earth. In all cases, the ground is either made firm with water, or trodden down or beaten flat with the spade after planting, so as to fix the roots firmly in the soil for the same reasons as nearly a similar plan is adopted in sowing seeds. Newly transplanted trees are frequently staked, but this is not essential if the roots are made firm, and indeed the tree is generally found to do best when the head is left at liberty to be gently agitated by the wind.

It is a great point, in all cases of transplanting, to preserve the epidermis or cellular integument of the fibrous roots and spongioles in a fleixble state; and for this reason, the greatest care is taken to keep them moist. This is the end in view in puddling or fixing by water in transplanting; and many planters always dip the roots of trees and shrubs in water before replanting. When a tree or shrub is taken up that is to be conveyed any distance, the roots should be wrapped up as soon as it is taken out of the ground, in wet moss, and covered with bast matting; and where moss cannot be procured, they should be dipped in very wet mud, and then matted up. Cabbage-plants are frequently preserved in this manner; and are conveyed, without any other overing to their roots than a cake of mud, to a considerable distance. In all cases where plants are taken up long before they are replanted, the roots should be kept moist by opening a trench, and laying the plants along it, and then covering their roots with earth. This gardeners call laying plants in by the heels. Where this cannot be done, and the plants are kept long out of the ground, their roots should be examined, and moistened from time to time; and before planting they should be laid in water for some hours, and afterwards carefully examined, and the withered and decayed parts cut off.

In removing large trees, care is taken to prepare the roots by cutting a trench round the tree for a year or two before removal, and pruning off all the roots that project into it. This is to answer the same purpose as transplanting young trees in a nursery; while the bad effects of contracting the range of the roots is counteracted, by filling the trench with rich fresh earth. The removal is also conducted with much care; and either a large ball of earth is removed with the tree, or the roots are kept most, and spread out carefully at full length, when the tree is replanted. Some planters, before removing trees, mark which side stood to the south, in order to replant them with the same side turned towards the sun; and this is sometimes done with young trees from a nursery. The reason is, that the tree having generally largest branches, and being always most flourishing, on the side exposed to the sun, it is thought that its vegetation might be checked, were a different side presented to that luminary, by the efforts it must make to accommodate itself to its new situation. On the other hand, however, it may be urged that changing the position of the plant, particularly while it is young, will be beneficial in preventing it from taking

Mimulus, Maurandya, Lophospermum

any particular bent, and in promoting the equal distribution of sap through all the branches.

Watering

A most essential branch of culture. It has been already fully explained that the seed cannot vegetate, and the plant cannot grow without water. Carbon, and all the other substances that form the food of plants, must be dissolved in water to enable the spongioles to take them up; and the spongioles themselves, unless they are kept moist, will soon lose their power of absorption. Nothing indeed can be more evident, even to a common observer, than the necessity that plants feel for water; if a mimulus or a pelargonium in a pot, for example, hang its head and droop its leaves, what an extraordinary and rapid effect is produced by giving it water! In an almost incredibly short time its leaves become firm, and its stem erect; and the plant is not only preserved from death, but restored to full health and beauty.

Watering appears an extremely simple operation, yet nevertheless there are several points relating to it that it is necessary to attend to. One of these is, never to saturate the soil. Water, to be in the best state for being taken up by the plants, should be kept in detached globules by the admixture of air; and it should be only slightly impregnated with nourishing matter from decaying animal or vegetable substances: for, as already observed, when fully saturated with nourishment, it becomes unfit for the food of plants. Nothing can be more admirably and wonderfully adapted for supplying plants properly with water than rain. In falling through the atmosphere, it is thoroughly mixed with the air, and in sinking into the soil it becomes slightly impregnated with nutritious qualities, which it is thus enabled to convey, in the most beneficial manner, to the plants.

It is a very common mistake, in watering, to pour the water down close to the stem of the plant. This is injurious in every respect. Water, when poured profusely on the collar of the plant, which is the point of junction between the root and the stem, is likely to rot, or otherwise seriously injure that vital part; while the spongioles, which alone can absorb the water, so as to benefit the plant, being at the extremity of the roots, are always as far removed from the stem as the nature of the plant will allow. Thus, the distance from the stem at which water should be given varies in different plants. In those that have tap-roots, such as the carrot, any many other culinary vegetables, the lateral fibrous roots are short, and the spongioles are comparatively near the stem; but in trees, and most plants having spreading roots, the spongioles are generally as far distant from the stem as the extremity of the branches; and the water, to be efficacious, should be given there.

The quantity of water to be given varies, not only according to the nature of the plant, but to the state of its growth. In spring, when the sap first begins to be in motion, and the young plant is every day unfolding fresh leaves or blossoms, it requires abundance of water; as it does when in flower, or when the fruit is swelling. In autumn, on the contrary, when the fruit is ripening, and in winter, when the plant is in a sate of perfect reset, very little water is necessary, and much is positively injurious, as being likely either to excite a morbid and unnatural action in the vessels, or even to bring on rottenness and decay. Water is necessary for seeds to induce them to germinate; but much of it is injurious to young plants when they first come up, as it unsettles their roots, and almost washes them away.

The roots, also, are at first too weak to imbibe water; and the plants feed on the nourishment contained in the cotyledons, or in the albumen of the seeds. It is when the second pair of leaves has opened that water is required, though it should at first be given sparingly. When the plant begins to grow vigorously, it requires more food; and if it be then kept too short of nourishment, it becomes stunted in its growth. The quantity of water requisite also depends on the kind of leaves that the plant unfolds. A plant with large broad leaves, like the tobacco, requires twice as much water as a plant with small pinnate leaves, like an acacia. Plants exposed to a strong light, also, require more than plants grown in the shade.

The time for watering plants varies according to the season. In spring and autumn it is best to water plants in the morning. But in summer, the usual time is the evening; while in winter, the very little that is required should be given in the middle of the day. Many persons object to watering their plants when the sun is upon them; but this is not at all injurious, so long as the water is not too cold, and is only given to the roots. Watering the leaves when the sun is upon them will make them blister, and become covered with pale brown spots wherever the water has fallen. It is much better to water plants during sunshine, then to suffer them to become too dry; as when the spongioles are once withered, no art can restore them. When plants have been suffered to become too dry, the ground should be loosened before watering it; and water should be given a little at a time, and frequently, till the plant appears to have recovered its vigour. A great deal of the good produced by watering depends on the state of the ground; as when the ground is hard and compact, it is very possible to throw a great quantity of water upon it without doing any service to the plants.

The kind of water used should also be considered. The best is pond-water, as it is always mixed with air, and is, moreover, generally impregnated with decayed animal and vegetable matter; and the worst is clear spring-water, as it is always cold, and is seldom impregnated with air, or with anything but some mineral substance, which, so far from doing good, is positively injurious to the plants.

Rain-water collected in open cisterns, and river-water, are both very suitable; and when only spring-water can be obtained, it should be exposed for some time to the air before using it. It is always advisable to have the water at least as warm as the plants to be watered; and for this reason the water to be used in hot-houses and green-houses is generally kept in an open vessel in the house some hours before using. In some cases, the water may be much hotter than the temperature in which the plants are grown and the effect of hot water, not heated to above 200°, in forwarding bulbs is astonishing; but is must be observed that it should never be poured on the bulbs, or on the leaves, but on the earth near the rim of the pot. Hot water is also very efficacious in softening seeds with hard coverings when soaked in it; and some of the seeds of the New Holland acacias will not vegetate in this country till they have been actually boiled for some minutes.

Delphinium

Fritillaria

CHAPTER IV

MODES OF PROPAGATION BY DIVISION, VIZ. TAKING OFF SUCKERS, MAKING LAYERS AND CUTTINGS, BUDDING, GRAFTING AND INARCHING.

PROPERLY speaking, there are only two modes of propagating plants, viz.: by seed and by division. The first raises a new individual, resembling the plant that produced the seed, as a child does its parent, but not perpetuating any accidental peculiarity; and the second method multiplies specimens of the individual itself. Species are propagated by seed, and new varieties are raised; but varieties are generally propagated by division, as they do not always come true from seed.

The modes of propagation, by division, are of two kinds:– those in which the young plants root in the ground, such as suckers, layers, and cuttings; and those in which they are made to root in another plant, as in budding, grafting, and inarching.

Suckers

Sending up suckers, forming offsets, and throwing out runners, are all natural ways of propagation that require very little aid from the hand of man; and if all plants produced these, nothing more would be required than to divide the offspring from the parent and replant it in any suitable soil. But only certain plants throw up suckers, such as the rose, the raspberry, the lilac, the English elm, &c.; offsets are only formed on bulbs, and runners are only thrown out by strawberries, brambles, and a few other pants; and thus these modes of propagation are extremely limited in practice. No plants produce suckers but those that send out strong horizontal roots; as the sucker is in fact a bud from one of these roots which has pushed it way up through the soil, and become a stem. As this stem generally forms fibrous roots of its own, above its point of junction with the parent root, it may in most cases, when it is thought necessary to remove it, be slipped off the parent and planted like a rooted cutting.

As, however, the nourishment it can expect to derive from its own resources will be at first much less than what it obtained from its parent, it is customary, when a sucker is removed, to cut in its head, to prevent the evaporation from its leaves being greater than its roots can supply food for. Sometimes, when the parent is strong, part of the horizontal root to which the sucker was attached is cut off and planted with the young plant.

Suckers of another kind spring up from the collar of the old plant, and when removed are always slipped or cut off with the fibrous roots that they may have made, attached. Offsets are young bulbs which form by the side of the old one, and merely require breaking off, and planting in rich light soil. Runners are shoots springing from the crown or collar of the plant, which throw out roots at their joints; and which only require dividing from the parent plant, and replanting in good soil, to make new plants.

Layers

Many plants, when kept in a moist atmosphere, having a tendency to throw out roots from their joints, the idea of making layers must have very early occurred to gardeners. When the roots are thrown out naturally wherever a joint of the shoot touches the moist ear, (as in the case with some of the kinds of verbena, which only require pegging down to make them form new plants,) layers differ very little from runners; but layers, properly so called, are when the art of the gardener has been employed to make plants throw out roots when they would not have done so naturally. The most common method of doing this is to cut half through, and slit upwards, a shoot from a growing plant, putting a bit of twig or pot-sherd between the separated parts; and then to peg down the shoot, so as to bury the divided joint in the earth; when the returning sap, being arrested in its progress to the main root, will accumulate at the joint, to which it will afford such abundance of nourishment, as to induce it to throw out a mass of fibrous roots, and thus to convert the shoot beyond it into a new plant, which may be separated from the parent, and transplanted.

The only art required is to contrive the most effectual means of interrupting the returning sap, so as to produce as great an accumulation of it as possible, at the joint from which the roots are to be produced. For this purpose, sometimes, instead of cutting the branch half through, a ring of bark is taken off, care being taken that the knife does not penetrate into the wood; and at others a wire is twisted firmly round the shoot, so as to pinch in the bark; or a knife or other sharp instrument is passed

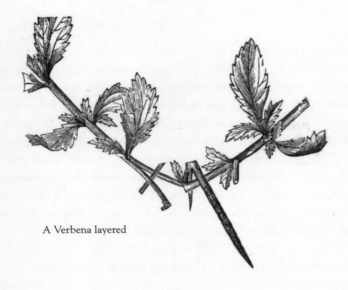

A Verbena layered

through the branch several times in different directions: in short, any thing that wounds, or injures the shoot, so as to throw an impediment in the way of the returning sap, and yet not to prevent the passage of the sap that is ascending, will suffice.

Layering is a very common mode of propagating plants; and in nurseries often every shoot of a tree or shrub is thus wounded and pegged down. In this case, the central root is called a stool, from the verb, *to stole*, which signifies the power most deciduous trees possess, of sending up new stems from their roots when cut down. The seasons for performing the operation of layering are during the months of February and March, before the new sap begins to rise, or in June or July after all the summer supply of ascending sap has risen; as at these seasons there is no danger of injuring the tree by occasioning an overflow of the ascending sap, which sometimes takes place when the tree is wounded while the sap is in active motion. In most cases the layers are left on twelve months, and in many two years, before they are divided from the parent plant, in order that they may be sufficiently supplied with roots. In nurseries, the ground is generally prepared round each stool by digging, and sometimes by manuring; and the gardener piques himself on laying down the branches neatly, so as to form a radiated circle round the stool, with the ends rising all round about the same height.

Chinese mode of layering

The Chinese method of layering, which consists in wounding a branch, and then surrounding the place with moist earth contained either in a flower-pot or a basket, is frequently adopted in the continental gardens; and it has the very great advantage of producing a young tree which will flower and fruit while yet of a very small size. It is generally applied to camellias, orange-trees, and magnolias; but it will do equally well for almost any other tree or shrub. When a plant is to be layered in this manner, a ring of bark is first taken off, and then a flower-pot is procured, open on one side, so as to admit the branch; and some moss being put at the bottom of the flower-pot, it is filled up with earth, and a piece of wood is placed inside the pot before the open part to prevent the earth from falling out. It may be fastened in its place by wires hung over a branch, or supported by four little sicks, tied to the pot with string. The

earth should be very moist before it is put into the pot, and if
the season be dry, it may be re-moistened from time to time.
When the layer is supposed to have rooted, a cut or rather notch
should be made in the branch below the pot, and afterwards it
may be cut off, and the young plant transferred with its ball of
earth entire, to another pot or the open ground. A simpler way

Chinese Mode of Layering

of performing this operation is using a piece of lead instead of a flower-pot. A modification of this plan was adopted by Baron Humboldt in South America. He provided himself with strips of pitched cloth, with which he bound moist earth round the branches of several of the rare and curious trees he met with, after first taking off a ring of bark; and when he returned to the same place some time after, he found rooted plants, which he brought to Europe.

Cuttings

Cuttings differ from layers in being removed without roots from the parent tree; and as the current of the ascending sap is stopped at once by this separation, they generally require shading, which layers do not; and also, occasionally, what gardeners call bottom heat, to induce them to throw out roots. The branches most suitable for making cuttings are those which grown nearest to the ground, especially those which recline on it, as they have always the greatest tendency to throw out roots; and even the erect side-shoots are considered preferable to those which grow at the upper part of the plant. The best season for making cuttings is summer, when the sap is in full motion; as the returning sap is then most likely to form the ring or mass of accumulated matter from which the new roots are to spring. It has been already mentioned under the head of layers, that it is from the joints only that roots can be expected to grow; and, accordingly, in making cuttings, the shoot is divided just below a joint; and it is generally reckoned best to choose a joint at he point of junction between the young wood and wood of the previous season. The cut should be quite smooth; as, if the shoot be bruised, the returning sap will not be able to reach the joint in a sufficient quantity to effect the desired end. Some plants are much more difficult to strike as cuttings than others; but some, such as the willow, the currant, the vine, &c., will throw out roots not only from the joints, but from every part of the stem. These plants do not require so much care as to cutting off at a joint; as they will throw out roots from whatever part may be put into the ground, but even they succeed best when properly prepared.

The cutting being taken off, and the division at the joint being made perfectly smooth, several of the leaves should be cut off close to the stem, with a sharp knife; and a hole being made in the soil, the cutting should be put in, and the earth pressed close to its extremity, or it will never strike out roots. This necessity of the part which is to send out roots being fixed firmly in the soil, has been already mentioned with regard to seeds, transplanted trees, and layers, and this necessity exists with equal or greater force with regard to cuttings. When these are made in a pot, the cutting will much more readily strike (as gardeners call its throwing out shoots), if it rest against the side of the pot, or even against the bottom.

Cuttings may be struck in the open ground, and in the common soil, without any covering; but these cuttings are only of those plants which strike readily. When struck in pots, it is customary to fill the pots half, or entirely full of silver sand, to prevent the stalk of the cutting from having too much moisture round it. Those cuttings which are most liable to be injured by moisture, such as heaths, &c., are struck in pots filled entirely

A Cutting of the Lemon-scented Verbena (*Aloysia citriodora*), prepared
for putting into the ground.

with sand; but as there is no nourishment to be derived from
sand, most cuttings do best with their lower end in earth, and
with only sand about an inch, or two inches deep, at the top of
the pot, to keep the stem dry, and to prevent it from rotting.

The cutting, when prepared, should be buried to about the
second joint, and two or three joints with leaves should be left
above the soil. A few leaves to elaborate the sap in the case of
herbaceous plants, or evergreen trees and shrubs, are essential;
for I have known very promising cuttings of petunias, which
had been some weeks in the ground, and which had thrown out
abundance of roots, entirely destroyed by some snails having

A Cutting of the China Rose (*Rosa indica*), prepared for putting into ground; it being observed that the leaves represented as shortened, are only drawn so for want of room in the page.

eaten all the leaves; and I am told that the case is by no means an uncommon one. Cuttings of delicate pants are generally covered with a bell-glass pressed closely on the earth, to keep a regular degree of moisture round the plants, and to prevent too rapid an evaporation; but some cuttings when thus treated are very apt to damp off, and require to have the glass taken off occasionally, and wiped. Cuttings of greenhouse plants, I have been told by practical gardeners, strike best when put into the pots as thickly as possible; and as they are generally well watered when first put into the ground, if covered with a close glass, they will very seldom require any watering afterwards.

As long as they continue looking fresh, they are doing well; and as soon as they begin to grow they should be transplanted into small thumb pots, and supplied moderately, but regularly, with water; changing the pots for larger ones as the plants increase in size, and according to their nature. Sometimes the pots are sunk into a hot-bed, to induce the cuttings to take root, and this is called applying bottom heat; and sometimes one flower-pot is placed within another a size or two larger, and the inner one filled with water (the hole at the bottom being first stopped with clay or putty), and the cuttings placed in the outer one. All these expedients are more or less efficacious; and the great object with all of them, is to excite and stimulate the plant.

Slips

When cuttings are made of the shoots from the root or collar of the plant, or of little branches stripped off with a small portion of the root or stem attached, they are called slips; and they require no other preparation than cutting off the portion of bark smooth and close to the shoot. Slips are generally taken off in March, but they will also succeed if made in autumn. Cuttings of succulent plants, such as of the different kinds of cacti, require to be dried for some time after they are made, but

placing them on a shelf in the sun. This is done to prevent the
wounded part from becoming rotten in the ground, as the sap
is very abundant, and in a very liquid state.

Pipings

Pipings are cuttings of pinks and carnations, and indeed are
applicable to all plants having jointed tubular stems. They are
prepared by taking a shoot that has nearly done growing, and
holding the root end of it in one hand, below a pair of leaves,
and with the other pulling the top part above the pair of leaves,
so as to separate it from the root-part of the stem at the socket
formed by the axils of the leaves, leaving the part of the stem
pulled off with tubular or pipe-like termination. Hence the
name of pipings; and when thus separated, they are inserted in
finely sifted earth or sand, and a hand-glass is fixed firmly over
them. Most florists cut off the tips of the leaves of pipings,
but others plant them entire; and the pipings grown apparently
equally well under both modes of treatment.

The principal points to be attended to in making cuttings
are, to cut off the shoot at a joint, without bruising the stem;
to make the cutting at a time when the sap is in motion; to fix
the end which is to send out roots, firmly in the soil; to keep
it in an equal temperature both as regards heat and moisture;
to cut off part of the leaves, and to shade the whole, so as
to prevent too much evaporation, without excluding the light,
which is wanted to stimulate the plant; to keep the soil moist,
but not too damp; and to pot off the young plants as soon as
they begin to grow.

Budding

Budding has been compared to sowing a seed; but it may rather be considered as making a cutting with a single eye, and inserting it in another tree, called the stock, instead of in the ground. A young shoot of the current year's wood is cut off in the latter end of July or August, or perhaps, if the season should be very moist, the first week in September; and incisions are made longitudinally and across, on each side, above and below a bud, so that the bud may be cut out, attached to an oblong pice of wood and bark, pointed at the lower end. The leaf is then taken off, but the footstalk is left on.

The next thing is to separate the bark with the bud attached from the wood; and on the nicety of this operation much depends, as if any wood be left in the bark the bud will not take; generally, however, if the sap be in a proper state of movement, the wood comes out easily, without leaving the smallest particle behind. The bud must be then examined below, that is, on the side that was next the wood; and if it appears fresh and firm, it is likely to take, but if it looks shrunk and withered, it had better be thrown away, as it will never grow. Slits longitudinal and across are then made in a shoot of the stock, generally near the fork of a branch; and the bark gently raised by the handle of the budding knife, which is purposely made thin and flat, while the piece of bark to which the bud is attached is slipped into the opening, and the bark of the stock closed over it. This is an operation that requires the greatest nicety and exactness; as unless the inner bark of the bud fits quite closely to the soft wood of the stock, it is in vain to hope that it willl take. The

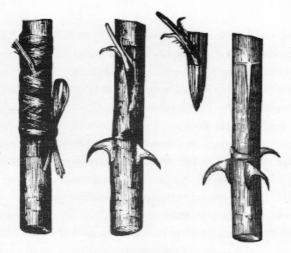

Mode of Budding a Rose-Tree.

operation is then completed by binding the two parts together
with a strand or strip of bast mat, which in the case of rose
trees is quite sufficient; but buds on apple and pear trees are
sometimes wrapped round with wet moss, which is tied on by
shreds of bast matting. In all cases, the strips of bast should be
left long enough to be tied with bows and ends, that the ligature
may be loosened, and tied again without deranging the position
of the bud, as soon as it begins to grow. The first sign of the
bud having taken, as it is called, is when the petiole of the leaf
that was left on when the leaf itself was cut off, drops, on being
very slightly touched with the finger; but the ligature should
not be loosend till the bud begins to throw out leaves; and then
it should be re-tied only a little slacker than before, until the

bud is firmly united with the stock.

In France, buds are only applied to a part of the stock from which a bud has been taken, so that the bud of the scion may exactly supply the place of the original bud of the plant. But this precaution, though certainly founded on reason, is seldom attended to in England.

Budding, though sometimes used for apples and pears, when the spring grafts have failed, is most commonly applied to roses: it is, however, occasionally used for inserting eyes in the tubers of the dahlia. The root of the dahlia consists of a number of tubers, collected together, and each of which should be furnished with an eye or bud at its summit, so as to form a ring round what is called the crown of the root, from which the stems of the plant are to spring. When the plant is to be propagated, the tubers are divided, and planted separately, and each that has a bud at its summit will send up a stem, and will become a new plant. Sometimes, however, it happens that several of the tubers are devoid of buds, and that others have more than one, and when this is the case, one of the buds is scooped out, and a notch being made in the top of the barren tuber to receive it, the bud is fitted in, and the point of junction covered with grafting wax. The tuber must then be planted in a pot with the budded part above the soil; and the pot plunged into a hot-bed till the bud begins to push, when the tuber may be planted out into the open ground.

What is called flute-grafting, is, in fact, a kind of budding; as it consists in taking a ring of bark, on which there is a bud, off a shoot; and then supplying its place with a ring of bark,

with a bud attached, from another tree: placing the suppositious bud as nearly as possible in the position of the true bud. Sometimes, however, this is not thought necessary; and the ring of bark is taken from any part of the stock; though it is always replaced by a ring of bark containing a bud from the scion. There are many other kinds of budding, but as the principles are the same in all, it is not necessary to details them here. The blade of the budding knife should be short, and curve outwards, to lessen the danger of wounding the wood when making the incisions.

The principal points to be attended to in budding, are, to choose a fresh healthy bud; to separate the bark to which it is attached, without wounding it, quite cleanly from the wood; to make a clear incision through the bark of the stock, and to raise it from the wood without wounding it; to press the bark containing the bud so closely to the wood of the stock that no air can remain between them; and to perform the operation in moist weather, not earlier than the last week in July, nor later than the first week in September. Of these points the most important are the joining closely the bark of the bud to the wood of the stock, and the performing the operation in moist, or at least in cloudy weather; and if these are attended to there is little doubt of success. When the young shoot begins to grow, it is usual to shorten the branches of the stock, so as to throw the whole vigour of the tree into the bud. It is singular to observe that even when the operation is most successful, no intimate union takes place between the bud and the stock: they grown firmly together, but they do not incorporate, and the point of union may always be distinctly traced.

It must always be remembered that a plant can only be budded on another plant of the same nature as itself; thus a peach may be budded on a plum, as they are both stone fruits, and both belong to the same section of the natural order Rosaceæ; but a peach can neither be budded on a walnut, which belongs to another natural order, nor even on a an apple or a pear, both of which, though belonging to the order Rosaceæ, are kerneled fruits, and are included in another section.

Grafting

Grafting differs from budding in its being the transfer of a shoot with several buds on it, from one tree to another, instead of only a single bud; and as budding has been compared to sowing seeds, so has grafting to making cuttings. The art of grafting consists in bringing two portions of growing shoots together, so that the liber or soft wood of the two may unite and grow together; and the same general principles apply to it as to budding. There are above fifty modes of grafting described in books, but only three or four are in common use.

In all kinds of grafting the shoot to be transferred is a called the scion, and the tree that is to receive it is called the stock; and it is always desirable, not only that the kinds to be united

should be of the same genus, or at least of the same natural
family, but that they should agree as closely as possible in their
time of leafing, in the duration of their leaves, and in their
habits of growth. This is conformable to common sense; as it
is quite obvious that unless the root send up a supply of sap at
the time the leaves want it, and only then, the graft must suffer
either from famine or repletion. For this reason, a deciduous
plant cannot be grafted on an evergreen, and the reverse. The
necessity of a conformity in the habit of growth, is strikingly
displayed in Mr. Loudon's *Arboretum Britannicum*, in a wood
engraving of a flowering ash grafted on a common ash, and
growing at Leyden; by which it is shown, that an architectural
column with its plinth and capital may be formed in a living
tree, where there is a decided difference in the growth of the
stock and the scion.

These examples show that no intimate union takes place
between the scion and the stock; and the fact is, that though
they grow together and draw their nourishment from the same
root, they are in every other respect perfectly distinct. The stock
will bear its own leaves, flowers, and fruit, on the part below the
graft; while the scion is bearing its leaves, flowers, and fruit,
which are widely different, on the part above the graft. Nay,
five or six grafts of different species on the same tree, will each
bear a different kind of fruit at the same time. This want of
amalgamation between the scion and the stock is particularly
visible in cases of severe frost, when the former is more tender
than the latter; as the graft is frequently killed without the stock
being injured. It is also necessary when grafted trees are for any

reason cut down, to leave a portion above the graft for the new shoots to spring from; as otherwise the proprietor will find his trees changed as if by magic, and instead of choice kinds only the common sorts left. A rather droll instance of this happened some years ago, in the neighbourhood of London: an ignorant gardener having a conservatory full of very choice Camellias, and wishing to reduce the plants to a more compact shape, cut them down for that purpose; when in due time he found, to his great confusion and dismay, that the choice Camellias had all vanished, and that he had nothing left but a number of plants of the common single red on which they had been grafted.

The proper season for grafting is in spring, generally in March and April; in order that the union between the scion and the stock may be effected when the sap is in full vigour. At this season a stock is chosen of nearly the same diameter as the scion, whether that stock be young tree, or merely a branch; and they are both cut so as to fit each other. One piece is then fitted on the other as exactly as possible; and if practicable, it is contrived that the different parts, such as the bark, soft wood, and hard wood, of the one, may rest on the corresponding parts of the other; and on the exactness with which this is done, the neatness of appearance of the graft depends. It is not, however, essential to the success of the operation, that all the parts of the scion should fit exactly on the corresponding parts of the stock, or even that the two trees should be of the same diameter, for if the bark and the soft wood correspond in any one point so as to unite, it is sufficient to make the graft take. As soon as the scion and the stock are properly fitted to each other, the parts are neatly bound together with a strand of bast mat steeped in water to make it flexible; and the bast is covered with a composition called grafting clay, which is put on to keep the absorbent vessels of the wounded parts moist, and capable of alternate contractions and dilations which will be necessary during the passage of the ascending and returning sap between the stock and the graft. These directions apply alike to all kinds of grafting; and the difference between the sorts refers principally to the manner in which the corresponding parts are cut to fit each other.

Whip or Tongue Grafting

Whip or tongue grafting is where both the stock and the scion are cut in a slanting direction so as to fit each other, and a little slit is made in the stock into which a tongue or projecting part cut in the scion fits. The head of the stock is then cut off in a slanting direction, slanting upwards from the part cut to receive the scion, and the two are bound closely together with a strand of bast mat, or wrapped in moss, and then covered with grafting clay. The part left on the stock in a slanting direction above the graft withers, and is cut off when the graft has taken. This is the kind of grafting generally practised in nurseries, and it is the most useful, as it does not require the scion and the stock to be of the same size.

Cleft grafting

Cleft grafting is where the scion is shaped at the extremity like a wedge, and a cleft is made in the stock to receive it. When this kind of grafting is practised with trees and shrubs, the head of

The common mode of Whip or Tonge Grafting.

the stock is cut off; but a modification of it is practiced with succulent plants, in which the end of the graft having been cut into the shape of a wedge, is inserted in a cleft or notch made in the side of the stock to receive it, and the line of junction is covered with grafting wax. The tubers of strong common dahlias may be grafted in the cleft manner with choice sorts, as may the tubers of the herbaceous paeonies with scions of the

tree-pæony. This last is very useful, as cuttings of the Paeonia
Moutan remain weak for several years, while roots grafted in
July or August will flower the following spring.

Crown grafting

Crown grafting resembles the last kind in requiring the head of
the stock to be cut off, but the scion is shaped at the extremity
like a wedge flattened on one side, and it is pushed in between
the bark and wood of the stock, with its flat side next the
wood, till it is stopped by a shoulder with which it is provided,
to prevent it going in too far. In Saddle Grafting the head of the
stock is cut off, and the extremity of the trunk is shaped like a
long wedge; a long slit then made in the scion, and the divided
parts are made to stand astride on the stock. The bark is then
pared off at the extremity, so that the two parts may fit quite
close; and a firm ligature is applied.

Herbaceous grafting

Herbaceous grafting is very badly named, as it gives the idea
of its being a kind of grafting applied to herbaceous plants;
whereas, in fact, it only means grafting with the brittle wood
of the current year, in opposition to common grafting, which
is always performed with firm wood, frequently of several
years' growth. Herbaceous grafting is now generally used for
trees of the pine and fir tribe, which, only a few years ago, it
was thought impossible to graft at all. The proper time for
this kind of grafting is when the young pine-shoots have made
about three parts of their growth, and are still so herbaceous as

to break readily between the fingers, like a shoot of asparagus. The shoot of the stock is then broken off about two inches below the point, and all the leaves stripped off for nearly two inches more, except two sheaths of leaves, which are left, one on each side, close to the top. The shoot is then split with a very thin knife between the sheaths of leaves left on, and the scion, having had its lower extremity prepared by stripping off the leaves, and cutting it into the shape of a wedge, is inserted as in cleft grafting, and the parts are bound together with list, or with a strip of thin woollen cloth. A cone of paper is then put over the whole to protect it from the sun and rain, and the graft is very seldom found to fail.

Sometimes this kind of grafting is applied to annual plants. The period chosen should be when the plant is in its greatest vigour, and is just going into flower. The flower stem is cut off close to a leaf, and a slit is made in the stem downwards. The scion is then taken off near the root of the plant, and the end, being cut into a wedge-shape, is inserted in the slit. The wound is afterwards bound up with strips of cloth spread with grafting wax, and the leaf taken great care of. When the graft begins to grown, this leaf and all the shoots above it are removed. In this manner artichokes have been grafted on cardoons, and cauliflowers on cabbages with great success. Tomatoes have also been grafted on potatoes, the potatoes perfecting their tubers, and the tomatoes their fruit, at the same time; and it is said that the ripening of the latter was much accelerated. This mode of grafting was invented by the Baron Tschoudy, a gentleman residing at Metz, and the principal point in it which requires

Mode of Inarching the Camellia.

Stock and Scion prepared for Inarching

attention, is the preserving a leaf, or two leaves, at the extremity of the stock, to serve as nurses to the graft.

Inarching, or Grafting by Approach

Though I have left this till last, it is in fact the most simple of all ways of grafting, and it is certainly the only one practiced by nature. In a natural forest, two branches rub against each other in windy weather, till the bark of both becomes wounded; a calm ensues, and, while it lasts, the wounded branches laying across each other adhere and grow together. Of this, which is called inosculation, examples in the beech, the hornbeam, and the oak, are given in Mr. Loudon's *Arboretum Brtiannicaum*; and it is probable that mankind derived the first idea of grafting from observing instances of this kind. Inarching, as practised in nurseries, closely resembles layering. A branch is bent and partly cut through, and the heel thus formed is slipped into a slit made downwards in the stock to receive it. The parts are then made to meet as exactly as possible, and are bound together with bast mat, and covered with grafting clay, as in common grafting.

In five or six months the union will be complete; and the inarched plant with be ready to be separated from the parent, which is done with a very sharp knife, so as to leave a clean cut, and not a bruised one. The head of the stock, if it was left on when the plant was inarched, is then cut away, and the plant is ready for removal. It is, however, customary to keep on the grafting clay and ligature for a few weeks, till the plant is firmly established. This mode of propagation is very commonly practised in spring (generally in March) with Camellias and Magnolias; and it is usual in nurseries to see a fine new kind of Camellia surrounded by a sort of frame, on which are several pots of stocks of the single are placed at different heights for the convenience of attaching to them different branches of the choice kind, to undergo the process of inarching. In most of these cases the head of the stock is retained, and the scion introduced at the side; but as soon as the graft has taken, and has thrown out a sufficient number of leaves to carry on the elaboration of the sap, all the branches of the original plant above the graft are cut away to strengthen the inarched one.

Camellias are also now frequently grafted in a manner first

practised in Belgium, but afterwards greatly improved in the
nursery M. Soulange Bodin at Fromont, near Paris, and which
has the advantage of producing flowering plants much sooner
than by any other plan. This mode of grafting, which is called
la greffe étouffée en placage, or *la greffe des Belges;* and is a kind
of side grafting, or rather of inarching. It consists in cutting off
a small portion of the bark of the stock with a very little wood
attached, from the side of the stem, or one of the branches,
leaving a leaf and a bud above it; and then cutting the scion into
a chisel shape, so as to fit the wound in the stock exactly, and
binding the two closely together with a strip of bast matting,
but without using any other covering. As soon as the operation
is finished, the pot containing the stock is laid horizontally
on a bed of dry and cold tan, or on a bed of dry moss, the
branches lying on the surface, and the pot being half buried in
the tan or moss; the grafted part being covered with a bell-glass,
stuffed round the bottom with the moss or tan so as to prevent
a particle of air from entering. This close covering is kept on for
a fortnight, three weeks, or a month, according to the season; a
the end of which time, the graft will be found perfectly united
to the stock. Air is then admitted to the graft by degrees, by
first loosening, and then removing the moss from the glass; the
glass itself is afterwards taken off, and the pots set erect.

The great points to be attended to in this mode of grafting,
are giving the plants bottom heat and covering them closely,
whence the name of *greffe étouffée,* as the plants appear almost
stifled for want of air. According to both modes, as soon as
the graft has taken, the leaf and bud of the stock above the

insertion of the scion, which were left on to draw up the sap, are cut off, and the plant is then in a fit state to be removed to the green-house, or any other place where it is to flower.

Grafting-clay and grafting-wax have been so frequently mentioned in the various operations of grafting and budding, that it seems necessary to say a few words on their composition. Common grafting-clay is made with any kind of stiff clay mixed with a fourth part of fresh horse-dung free from litter, and a portion of cut hay; a little water is sprinkled on the mass, and the whole is beaten together several times a-day for about a week, till the ingredients are thoroughly amalgamated. The common French grafting-clay, or Onguent de Ste Fiacre, is composed of equal parts of stiff clay and cow-dung; but a superior kind, recommended by M. De Cadolle, is composed of one pound of cow-dung, half a pound of pitch, and half a pound of yellow wax. Grafting-wax is generally made of equal parts of turpentine, bees'-wax, and resin, with a little tallow, melted together, and thoroughly incorporated. This is thinly spread on pieces of coarse cotton, and used in strips like cerecloth. In grafting trees that have a soft and delicate bark, fine moss and cotton wool tied on with a ligature of bast mat, are better than anything else, and they are generally quite sufficient for every purpose in which grafting is employed by ladies. A new composition has been lately invented, made with caoutchouc, which is said to be very efficacious, but I have never seen it tried.

The essential points to be attended to in grafting are choosing a stock and a scion that correspond in nature and in habits of growth; cutting the parts to be united so as to fit exactly, and leave no vacuity between; taking care that the soft wood of the scion shall always rest on the soft wood of the stock, as it is between these parts that the union is to be effected; binding the parts closely together, and covering them so as to prevent them from becoming so dry as to shrink apart, in which case the vessels would wither and become incapable of uniting.

Uses of grafting and budding

The obvious use of grafting is to propagate varieties that cannot so easily be continued by seed, and that will not strike by cuttings. There is, however, another use nearly as important; and this is to make plants flower and fruit sooner than they would otherwise do. There are many plants that only flower at the extremity of their shoots; and these plants, when tender, would require enormous plant-houses before they would be thrown into flower or fruit. To remedy this inconvenience, a method has been devised of cutting off the tips of the shoots and grafting them; and then, after they have grown for some time, cutting off the tips again and regrafting them, by means of which flowers are at length produced on plants of quite small size. The same method is applied in Paris to exotic fruit-trees, to throw them into fruit; and it has been tried with success with rose-apple (Eugenia Jambos), the mango, &c. In common nurseries, the fruit of new seedling apples is obtained much sooner by grafting their shoots on common apple stocks, than by leaving the young plants to nature; and this plan is also practised at Brussels by Prof. Van Mons, to test his seeding-pears.

Delphinium

CHAPTER V

PRUNING, TRAINING, PROTECTING FROM FROST, AND DESTROYING INSECTS.

PRUNING appears, at first sight, a most laborious and unfeminine occupation; and yet perhaps there is no operation of gardening which a lady may more easily accomplish. With the aid of a small and almost elegant pair of pruning shears, which I procured from Mr. Forrest, of the Kensington Nursery, I have myself (though few women have less strength of wrist) divided branches that a strong man could scarcely cut through with a knife. The only thing to be attended to is to choose a pair of pruning shears with a sliding joint, so as to make what is called a draw-cut; in order that the branch may be divided by a clean cut, and not bruised on the side next the plant, and also to leave a somewhat sloping section. When a branch is pruned, it should also be cut as near to a bud as can be done without injuring the bud itself; or, to speak more definitely, not more in length than the branch is thick should be left beyond the bud. The cut should slope downwards from the bud to prevent the water lodging in the angle; and also that the sun and air may have their full influence in exciting the bark to cover the wound. When a long piece of branch, or what gardeners call a snag, is left beyond the bud, it withers, from there being no leaves beyond it to carry on the circulation of the sap; and it thus not only becomes a deformity, but very often

seriously injures the tree by rotting, and infecting the fruit-bearing branch to which it is attached.

According to the usual method of pruning with a knife, the gardener holds the branch in his left hand, below the part that is to be removed; and then, holding the knife firmly with the thumb at the back of the blade, he makes a strong cut upwards, and from him, so as to remove the branch with a single stroke, and to leave a slanting section. This operation, however, requiring strength as well as skill, it will generally be safer for a lady to use only her pruning shears, which will be sufficient to cut through the largest branch that a lady would be able to remove; or to use a pair of garden scissors fixed to a pole, which may be lengthened or taken to pieces like a fishing-rod, as is practised by Captain Mangles. The scissors are strong and sharp, and are made to act by means of a long cord, which passes through rings down the side of the pole. The principal use of these scissors is to remove dead roses, &c., but they will also cut off a branch of dead wood, &c. When a large branch is to be removed, it is generally necessary to cut a notch out of it on each side, and then to divide the remainder with a pruning knife, or a small saw, but this is an operation that most ladies will prefer leaving to a gardener. In all cases, the great art of pruning consists in making a clean sharp cut, so as to leave the bark in a healthy state to make an effort to cover over the wound, and in pruning sufficiently near a bud not to leave any dead wood.

The time for pruning is either early in spring, after all danger
from frost, but before the sap has begun to move; or in winter,
after the movement of the sap for the summer has ceased.
Summer pruning is also necessary with some trees; but, generally
speaking, it should be confined to rubbing off all buds, which
would produce unnecessary shoots, as soon as they appear.
This operation is called disbudding, and it is highly efficacious
in sparing the strength of the tree. Many persons pinch off the
points of those shoots which appear to be running too much
to wood, but as this only excites the branch to throw out fresh
shoots, it is much better to strip the superfluous branches of
their leaves as they appear; and as, when thus treated, they can
produce no buds for want of leaves, their growth will be checked
without injuring the tree, and they may be safely removed in the
winter pruning. The vine is very apt to bleed when pruning has
been delayed too late; and in very strong vigorous plants, the
ascending sap sometimes drops from the branches like rain. The
French, very poetically, call these drops the tears of the vine.

The uses to which pruning is applied are various; but most
commonly it is intended either to improve the form of the
tree, or to make it bear more flowers and fruit than it otherwise
would do; it is also used for removing diseased or broken
branches; and, in cases of transplanting, for proportioning the
head to the roots.

Pruning to improve the form of a tree in pleasure-grounds
is only required in those cases where trees have grown under
unfavourable circumstances, and where they have been too much
drawn up, or distorted in any manner; but in useful plantations it

is necessary to prepare trees for the purposes for which they are intended. Thus, for example, a tree intended for timber, should have its side-branches taken off while they are quite young, in order that the wounds may soon heal over, and not leave loose knots to weaken or disfigure the wood; while a tree intended for a screen should be allowed ample space for its branches to spread from the ground upwards, and then they should only be shortened at their extremities, to make them throw out short branches near the tree. In pleasure-grounds the principal object is generally either to preserve the shape of the tree or shrub, so that it may form an agreeable object on a lawn; or to let it combine in a group with others, either for ornament, or to serve as a screen or shelter. In the first case, it is obvious that no pruning is requisite, but to remove dead, diseased, or unsightly branches; and in the second, the pruning must depend upon the shape the tree is required to take to group well with the others planted near it.

Pruning to produce flowers or fruit has in view two objects: first to cut off all superfluous wood, so as to throw the strength of the tree into the fruit-bearing branches; and secondly, to admit the sun and air into the interior of the tree. In both cases the attention of the pruner must be directed to thinning out weak and crowded shoots; and to keeping both the sides of the tree well balanced, in order that the circulation of the sap may be equal throughout. This will preserve the general health of the tree, at the same time that it throws the sap into the proper channels; and the fruit will be produced in as much abundance as can be done without injuring the tree. It should never be forgotten, that to effect permanent improvements, nature should be aided, not overstrained; and that all extraordinary exertions are succeeded by a period of feebleness and languor, or, if the exertion be continued too long, by death. Thus, all cases of pruning and training to produce fruit should never be pushed too far, as though, by occasioning an extraordinary deposit of the returning sap in some particular part, that part may be forced into fruit, the unnatural deposit cannot fail in the end to engender disease.

Sometimes a tree, from being supplied with more food than it can digest, or from some other cause, has a tendency to produce what the English gardeners call water-shoots, and which the French call gourmands. These are strong, vigorous-growing branches, which are sent up from the main trunk of the tree, but which do not produce either flowers or fruit; and which, consequently, if the tree be full of wood, should be removed as soon as their true character is discovered. If, however, the tree have too little wood in the centre, or if it appear exhausted by too much bearing, these branches should be spared, as they will serve admirably both to fill up any blanks that my have been left in the training, and to strengthen the trunk and roots by the quantity of rich returning sap, which they will send down from their numerous leaves. A certain quantity of leaves and barren branches are essential to the health of every tree; and the fruit grower who consults his own interest, should cherish them, instead of grudging the sap required for their support. Whenever there is not a sufficient quantity of leaves to elaborate the sap, the fruit that ought to have been nourished by its rich juices, becomes flaccid and insipid; its skin grows tough instead of crisp; and if the deprivation of leaves has been carried to excess, the fruit never ripens, but withers prematurely, and falls off. Pruning, at the best, is a violent remedy; and, like all other violent remedies, if carried further than is absolutely necessary, it generally ends by destroying.

Training

Training is intimately connected with pruning, and like it should always be used with caution. A trained tree is a most unnatural object, and whatever care may be taken of it, there can be no doubt that training shortens its life by many years. The principal object of training is to produce from a certain number of branches a greater quantity of fruit or flowers than would grown on them if the plant were left in its natural state; and this is effected by spreading and bending the branches, so as to form numerous depositions of the returning sap, aided, where the plant is trained against the wall, by the shelter and reflected heat which the wall affords. Thus the points to be attended to by the gardener in training, are the covering of the wall, so that no part of it may be lost; the bending of the branches backwards and forwards, so that they may form numerous deposits of the returning sap; and the full exposure of the fruit-bearing branches to the sun and air. For these purposes the gardener shortens the long shoots, to make them throw out side-branches, with which he covers his walls, never suffering them to cross each other, but letting each be as much exposed to the influence of the air and light as is consistent with a necessary quantity of leaves; and he bends them in different directions to throw them into fruit. These general principles are common to all fruit-trees, but of course they must be modified to suit the habits of the different kinds. Thus, for example, some trees, such as the fig and the pomegranate, only bear on the extremities of their shoots; and, consequently, if their shoots were continually shortened, these trees would never bear at all; other trees, such as the apple and the pear, bear their fruit on short projecting branches, call spurs; and others at intervals on nearly all the branches, and close to the wall. All these habits should be known to the gardener, and the modes of training adopted which will be suitable to each. Training flowers should also be regulated by a knowledge of the habits of the plants; but it consists principally in checking their over-luxuriance of growth, and tying them to stakes or wooden frames. In all kinds of training, neatness is essentially requisite, and any departure from it is exceedingly offensive. Where the hand of art is so evident as it is in training, we require excessive neatness to make amends for the loss of the graceful luxuriance of nature.

The operation of training against a wall is performed by the aid of nails and shreds; the shreds being narrow oblong pieces of list or cloth, put round the branches, and attached to the wall by nails driven in with a hammer. Care should be taken that the pieces of list are long enough to allow the free passage of the sap, and yet not so long as to permit the branch to be so agitated by the wind as to bruise itself against the wall. The nails should also never be so driven in so as to wound or corrode the bark; and when driving in the nails, the gardener should be very careful not to bruise the branch with his hammer. The shreds should be broad enough not to cut the bark, and yet not so broad as to cover the buds; and they should, as much as possible, be of some uniform and dark colour. As few shreds should be used as are sufficient to attain the end in view; but these should be very firmly attached, as nothing gives a more gloomy picture of misery and desolation in a garden, than trees that once were trained, having become detached, and hanging drooping from the wall. Sometimes wires are fastened to walls, to which the plants are tied with strands of bast mat; the strand, after it is put round the branch and wire, being gently twisted between the finger and thumb, in order that it may make a firm knot without tearing or weakening the ligament. Climbing shrubs are tied to the pillars of a verandah, or to trellis work, in the same manner; as are also flowers to sticks, or slight wooden or wire frames, with the exception that, in their case, the bast does not require twisting.

Protecting from frost

An essential part of culture to a lady gardener, particularly in so uncertain a climate as that of England. Not only the blossoms of peaches and nectarines, and those of other early flower fruit-trees, are liable to be injured by the spring frosts; but those of the tree pæony, and other beautiful shrubs, are frequently destroyed by them; and, unfortunately, many of the modes of protection, by knocking off and bruising the blossoms, are almost as injurious as the frosts that they are intended to guard against. Twisting a straw-rope round the trunk of the tree, and putting its ends into a bucket of water, is certainly a simple method, and it has been recommended as a very efficacious one. What a mat is used to

Paeonia

protect wall trees, it does perhaps least injury to the blossoms, when curtain rings are sewed to its upper end, and it is hung by these on hold-fasts, or large hooks, driven into the upper part of the wall. To make it more secure, particularly in windy weather, it may be tied on the sides with bast to nails driven into the wall; and a broad moveable wooden coping should rest on the hold-fasts, and cover the space between the mat and the wall, to prevent injury from what are called perpendicular frosts.

Camellias and many half-hardy shrubs may be protected by laying straw or litter round the roots; as the severest frosts seldom penetrate more than a few inches into the ground. Even in the severe winter of 1837-8, the ground was not frozen at the depth of ten inches. Tree paeonies, and other tender shrubs, that are in a growing state very early in the spring, may be protected by coverings of basket-work, which are sufficiently large and light to be lifted off in fine days Hand and bell glasses, sea-kale pots, and wooden frames covered with oiled paper, are all useful for protecting small plants.

It is astonishing how very slight a covering will often suffice to protect a plant from frost, if the covering be over the top of the plant, even though the sides be exposed; while, on the contrary, a warm covering in front of the plant will fail to save it, if the top be exposed to the perpendicular frosts. Protecting the roots and collar, is a most important point, and few half-hardy trees and shrubs will be seriously injured, if the ground over their roots is covered a few inches deep with straw or dead leaves. Every lady should have two or three hand-glasses, of different sizes, always at her disposal, even during summer, for the convenience

of sheltering newly transplanted plants, &c.; and for winter use
she should have several beehive-like covers, each with a handle
for lifting it, formed of plaited rushes or some similar materials,
which may easily be made by poor women and children in
country places, under the direction of a lady; and which will be
a charitable mode of employing them.

Insects, and Snails, and Slugs

The terror of all gardeners; and the destruction they effect in
some seasons in small gardens is almost beyond the bounds
of credibility. Birds do comparatively little injury, and indeed
all the soft-billed kinds (which fortunately include most of the
sweetest songsters) do good. The willow and common wrens, the
black-cap, the nightingale, the redstart, all the warblers and fly-
catchers, the swallows and martins, the wagtails, the wryneck,
the tom-tit, the fern owl or night jar, and many others live almost
entirely on insects, and destroy great numbers every year: while
the blackbird and the thrush, the robin and the sparrows, though
they devour a portion of the fruit, destroy insects also. All birds
may indeed be safely encouraged in small gardens near towns, as
they will do much more good than injury; and a few cherries and
currants are a cheap price to pay for their delightful songs.

As it is the larvæ only of insects, with very few exceptions that
do injury to vegetation, many persons never think of destroying
them in any other state; forgetting that every butterfly that we see
fluttering about may lay thousands of eggs and that if we wait till
these eggs have become caterpillars, irreparable mischief will be
done to our plants before they can possibly be destroyed.

Whenever a butterfly is seen quietly sitting on the branch of a tree, in the day-time, it will generally be found to be a female, that either just laid, or, what is more probable, is just about to lay her eggs. As soon as the eggs are laid, the butterfly generally dies; and where dead butterflies are found, search should always be made for their eggs. In summer, a little oblong chrysalis, the colour of which is yellow, with black bands, will frequently be found hanging from the gooseberry-bushes; and whenever it is seen it should be destroyed. This chrysalis is the pupa of the magpie moth, the caterpillar of which frequently strips the gooseberry-bushes of all their leaves in spring, and thus renders their fruit worthless in summer.

The lackey caterpillar is another very destructive insect. These creatures, which are curiously striped, like the tags on a footman's shoulder, (whence their name,) assemble together in great numbers, and covering themselves with a web, completely devour the epidermis and parenchyma of the leaf on which they have fixed themselves; they then draw another leaf to them, which they also devour, and then another, till the greater part of the leaves of the tree they have attacked, present a fine lace-like appearance, as though they have been macerated. Did all these insects live to become moths, they would completely destroy not only our gardens, but our forests, as they feed on almost every different kind of tree; but with that beautiful arrangement by which all the works of our Great Creator are balanced equally with each other, and none allowed to predominate, these insects are such favourite food for birds, that not a hundredth part of them are suffered to reach maturity. The eggs of the lackey moth are often found fixed on a naked twig, in winter, looking like a bracelet of hard beads, and adhering so firmly together, that the whole bracelet may be slipped off entire.

The cabbage butterflies are also very destructive in the larva state. The caterpillars are soft, of a pale whitish green, and very active, leaping about in the hand when taken; and the chrysalis, which is also green, looks as if it were swathed up like a mummy. The caterpillar of the beautiful little ermine moth is a gregarious feeder, like the lackey caterpillar, and is nearly as destructive; and it is the more necessary to mention this because the moth itself is so small, so delicate, and so quiet, that no one unacquainted with its habits would think of killing it as an injurious insect.

The leaf-rollers, the saw-flies, and the gnats which occasion the oak-galls, are all very destructive. The leaves of the rose-tree are often found marked, in summer, with pale-brown zigzag lines, with a narrow black line running down the middle of each. These lines are the work of a very small orange-coloured caterpillar, not more than two lines long, that lives on the parenchyma of the leaf; and the pale brown mark is occasioned by the epidermis drying where the pulp beneath it has been removed. The moth is called the red-headed pigmy, and it is so small as not to measure more than two lines and a half broad, when its wings are fully expanded. The "worm i' th' bud" of the rose, is the maggot or grub of one of the kinds of saw-fly; a beautiful transparent-winged creature that no one would suspect of springing from such a frightful-looking maggot. But of all the insects that infest the rose, the most destructive are the aphides. These little green flies cover the tender leaves and buds of the young shoots in myriads, and are extremely difficult to destroy, without spoiling the appearance of the shoots that have been attacked by them.

Tobacco-water is an excellent remedy, if not too strong. It should be made by steeping half-a-pound of the best tobacco in a gallon of hot water; and as soon as the infusion has become cold, the young shoots should be dipped in it, and suffered to remain a few seconds, after which they should be immediately washed in clean water before they are suffered to dry. If this be done carefully, the insects will be destroyed, and yet the shoots will remain uninjured. Lime-water may also be tried if not more lime be used than the water will hold in solution; as unless the water be quite clear in appearance, when applied, the plant will be very much disfigured with the white stains of the lime.

Another means of getting rid of all noxious insects, is to fumigate them with tobacco; and the best way of doing this is by a small brass fumigator, applied to one of the patent blowers. The fumigator is filled with loose tobacco, which is lighted, and the brass tube is then screwed on the blower, and the fume gently spread through the green-house, or among the plants. By putting a little of the moxa or Spanish tinder among the tobacco, or using it alone, caterpillars, butterflies, snails, &c., may be stupified, when they will fall from the branches, and may be gathered up and destroyed. There are also several kind of fumigating bellows. An excellent preventative remedy is to wash the stems and branches of deciduous rose-trees in winter, with water heated to 200°, or with a mixture of strong tobacco-water and soft-soap; cleaning the branches well at the same time with a soft brush. The American blight which infests apple-trees is another species of aphis, and may be destroyed in the same manner.

Besides the insects already enumerated, there are several kinds of beetles, which devour plants both in the larva and perfect state. Of these, the cockchafer remains in the larva state four years, and is one of the most destructive insects known; it is the celebrated *ver blanc* of the French. The rose beetle, or rose chaffer (Cetonia aurata), is extremely beautiful, from its splendid wing cases of burnished green and gold, and these beetles, notwithstanding their shape, which looks too heavy and clumsy for flying, may frequently, in hot summer weather, be seen upon the wing, making a loud buzzing noise. When taken up in the hand they draw up their feet, and appear to be dead; but, after having been handled and even tossed about for some time, they will, if a favourable opportunity appears to offer, suddenly spread out their wings and buzz away, leaving their captor too much astonished to be able to make any effort to retain them. Several of these insects may often be found in one rose; but they are supposed to be only engaged in sucking the honey from the flower, and not injuring it. They undergo their transformations in the ground, and the grubs are supposed to live entirely on little bits of rotten wood. Besides the insects already mentioned, the various kinds of weevils, and wire-worm, the thrips, the red spider, or rather mite (Acarus telarius), various kinds of tipula, or Gaffer long-legs, wood-lice, and earth-worms, are all found on plants, and are all more or less injurious to them. In the general destruction of insects, the Lady-bird should always be spared, as, both in its larva and its perfect state, it lives on the larvæ of the green fly, or aphis.

Snails and Slugs

Snails and slugs are more destructive to vegetation than any kind
of insect; and they are still more difficult to get rid of. There is
a very small grey slug, that is peculiarly injurious to plants in
pots; the large grey slug is also very destructive, and the common
garden snail. The beautifully banded snail (Helix nemoralis) is,
however, supposed to live partly on earth-worms, and the shell
slug (Testacella scutella) lives entirely on them. The usual modes
of entrapment snails, slugs, and wood-lice, are laying down slices
of raw potatoes or cabbage leaves at night, and examining them
before the dew is off the plants in the morning.

As, however, this requires very early rising, a more convenient
method is to lay a few flower pots upon their sides, near the places
where the snails have committed their ravages; and the snails,
which can neither move nor feed unless the ground be wet with
dew or rain, will generally be found to take refuge in the flower
pots from the heat of the sun. They are likewise often found in
the middle of the day, sticking against walls under ivy, or in box
edgings. In gardens very much infested with snails, search should
be made in winter among all the ivy and box in the gardens; and
all the snails found in a torpid state should be destroyed. This,
though some may escape, will effectually prevent them from
becoming numerous; and, as the eggs are not laid till April or
May, care should be taken, before that season, to destroy all the
snails that can be found. The eggs are round, almost transparent,
and of a bluish white, like opal; and they are always found in
small clusters, buried in the ground.

Anemone

Lilium

CHAPTER VI

WINDOW GARDENING, AND THE MANAGEMENT OF PLANTS IN POTS IN SMALL GREEN-HOUSES

THE management of plants in rooms is extremely difficult, from the want of proper light and most air: though this latter want may, in some measure, be obviated, by opening the window in front of which the plants stand, whenever circumstances will permit. It should never be forgotten that moist air is almost as essential to plants as water; and that they are seriously injured by being forced to inspire air at their breathing pores that is in too dry a state for them. I have often observed the healthy appearance of plants belonging to cottagers; and I believe it arises principally from the habit that most poor people have, of setting their plants out in the rain whenever there is a shower. This not only clears the leaves of dust, and opens the stomata or breathing pores, but gives the plant abundance of fresh air. Without a sufficiency of air and light, plants will soon become weak and sickly, and their leaves will turn yellow; but if a little fresh air be given to them every day when the temperature is not too cold, they will grown nearly as well in a room as in a green house.

Another reason why plants kept in rooms are generally unhealthy, is, that they are watered in a very irregular manner. Sometimes they are suffered to become so dry that the mould in which they grow will crumble under the pressure of the finger, and the spongioles of the roots are quite withered; and then a profusion of water is given to them, quite cold from the pump, though they have probably been standing in a temperature of from 60° to 70°. As a climax, part of this water is suffered to remain in the saucer for a day or two, till even the healthy part of the roots is thoroughly chilled, and the plant, if of a delicate nature, is destroyed. The reverse of all this should be the case. The plant should never be suffered to become so dry as to have the mould in a crumbling state; but if such a circumstance has been suffered to occur, it should be well watered with warm water of at least the temperature of the room, and better if rather warmer. Enough of this water should be given to fill the saucer; in order that every part of the mould and of the roots may imbibe some benefit from the moisture; but as soon as this has been done, the pot should be lifted out of the saucer, and the water thrown away, as nothing can be more injurious to the roots of most plants, than to have the pot they grown in kept standing in water. There are, however, some exceptions to this rule, such as all the kinds of Mimulus, the Hydrangea, Calla etihiopica, and some kinds of Calceolaria. All these, and all marsh plants, require abundance of water, and will not flower well unless the saucer be kept half full, though the water should be changed every day.

It is also a common fault to put plants kept in rooms, into too large pots; or, as the gardeners express it, to over-pot them. This has always a bad effect. If the soil be good, and not over-watered, the plants will indeed grow rapidly; but it will be to produce leaves and branches instead of flowers: and if the soil be over-watered, the mass of soddened soil round the roots has the same effect upon them as stagnant water in the saucer. The soil should always be in such a state as to admit air with the water to the roots; and this it cannot do when it becomes a blackened paste by being saturated with water. At the same time, frequent repotting is often absolutely necessary to keep the plants in a dwarf compact habit of growth, and to prevent them from being drawn up. The way in which gardeners ascertain when repotting is necessary, is by turning the plant out of its pot with the ball of earth attached; and if they find the roots look white round the outside of the mould, then the plant should be transferred to a larger pot, but only one size larger: afterwards it may be repotted again if necessary, but always to a pot only a little larger than the one it was taken from. By persevering in this mode of treatment for some time, and never advancing more than one size at a time, a plant may be grown to a large size, and made to produce abundance of flowers; while by the contrary treatment, that is, suffering it to remain in a very small pot, or shifting it suddenly into a very large one, the stem will become weakened and elongated, and the flowers will be few and very poor. In short, on the skilful management of repotting, or shifting, as the gardeners call it a great deal of the art of growing plants in pots depends.

The best soil for plants in pots is generally peat mixed with vegetable mould and sand; and the pots should be filled nearly a quarter of their depth with little bits of broken pots, called potshreds, so as to ensure complete drainage. When plants are shifted, they are turned out of their old pots with the balls of earth entire; the roots are then examined, and if any are wounded or decayed, they should be cut off. The new pot, having had a layer of potshreds placed at the bottom with a little earth, the plant is placed in the centre, so that the bole or collar may be just above the level of the rim, and the new earth is put in, and the pot being shaken to make it settle, the plant is then slightly watered, and set aside in the shade for the rest of the day. Plants should never be repotted when in flower; the best time is indeed when they are growing, before their flower buds begin to swell, as, when the flower buds have appeared, they should be allowed to remain undisturbed till the flowering season is completely over. Sometimes the soil in a pot looks black, and covered with moss. When this is the case, the plant should be turned out of the pot, and the black sodden earth shaken off the roots, which should be cut in, and should have all their decayed parts removed. The plant should then be repotted in another pot of the same, or nearly the same size as the one it was taken from, which should be well drained, and filled up with a compost of vegetable mould, sand, and peat. Thus treated, and only moderately but regularly watered with warm water, which should never be allowed to stand in the saucer, the plant will sooner recover: and if judiciously pruned in, if it has become elongated, it will become handsome, and what gardeners call well grown.

Another objection to growing plants in rooms is the great difficulty that exists in keeping them clear of insects; particularly the Aphis, or green fly, and the kind of mite (Acarus telarius) commonly called the red spider. These are generally destroyed by fumigating them with some kind of fumigating bellows. Washing with a syringe, and abundance of water, is, however, probably a better mode; as it has been often observed that neither the green fly nor the red spider will ever infest a plant that is frequently syringed.

Flower-pots

Flower pots are of many different kinds, but the common red earthenware are decidedly the best, because they are the most porous, and consequently do not retain the moisture so as to be injurious to the plants they contain. They are of various sizes, which are designated by the number made out of a certain quantity of clay called a cast. Thus the larger size, which is a foot and a half in diameter, is called a two, because there are only two made out of a cast; and the smallest-numbered size, which is only two inches in diameter, is called a sixty, because there are sixty pots made out of one cast. When I was in my gardening noviciate, I used to be very puzzled when I was told that rooted cuttings should be potted in thumbs or in sixties, and that a plant which required transplanting, should be put in a twelve, or en eight.

Thumbs are still smaller pots than sixties, for there are eighty to the cast; but as they are seldom used, they are not described by their number, but they are called thumb-pots, because they will not hold more than a large sized thumb. Besides the common flower-pots, there are double pots, one of which has been sent me by Capt. Mangles, which are very useful for balconies, as the roots of the plants are very apt to be injured, by the outside of the pot in which they grown being dried by the wind, or heated by the sun. When double pots are used, the interstice between the pots should be stuffed with moss kept moist.

China, or any kind of glazed pots, may also be used for balconies, as he material of which they are composed does not permit evaporation; but they should always be filled at least a third of their depth with broken crocks, or potshreds, to ensure drainage. A very elegant flower-pot, manufactured in Derby, as has been lately presented to me by Mrs. Booth, which combines the beautiful form of a vase, with all the convenience of the common flower-pot and saucer. These flower-pots are made of the common red porous earthenware, and they may, of course, be of any desirable size. All pots should be well drained, by having a layer of potshreds at the bottom, to prevent the hole from becoming choked up with the earth pressing against it; and hair-rooted plants, such as heaths, and most of the Australian shrubs, should have the pot filled to a third of its depth with potshreds. Succulent plants, such as the cacti, and mesembryanthemums, should be drained with cinders; as the potshreds, being of a porous material, would retain too much moisture for their roots.

The management of plants in a small green-house differs very little from that of plants in rooms. Whenever the weather will permit, air should be given, if only for half an hour in the middle of the day. The house should be kept clean, and free from dead leaves; and the plants should not be too much crowded. Nothing can look worse than pale sickly green-house plants, drawn up to an unnatural length, and so weak that their stems will not stand upright without the aid of a stick. When green-houses are crowded with plants, some of which are too far from the light this must be the case; and when it, it is quite hopeless to expect either healthy plants or fine flowers. Though it is adviseable to have saucers to the pots of plants kept in rooms, for the sake of cleanliness, it is much better for those kept in the green-house to be without them. All persons having a great number of plants in pots, should be provided with a small watering-pot, having a very long spout, for the convenience of reaching the different pots; and care should be taken to give water to each pot in succession, but resting the spout of the watering-pot in turn on each. The watering-pot may have roses of two or three different kinds, to screw on as wanted.

As different green-house plants require a somewhat different treatment, the following directions for the management of a few of the most popular may be useful to my readers.

Camellias

The Camellia is a plant which requires abundance of water, and is yet soon killed by suffering stagnant moisture to remain about the roots . When grown in pots there should be abundant drainage; that is, the pots should be nearly a quarter filled with potshreds. The soil should be peat-earth, and sand, which may be mixed with a little vegetable mould, if it is desired to have the plants of very luxuriant growth; and the plants should be potted high, so as to let the collar of the plant be quite above the rim of the pot. The pots should not have saucers, or if they have for the sake of cleanliness, the water should be carefully poured out of them immediately after the plants have been watered. The plants should be watered abundantly every day while their flower-buds are swelling; as, if this be neglected, the buds are very apt to drop off. When the flowers begin to expand, the watering is not of so much consequence, though it should be continued in moderate quantities; and abundance should be again given when the plants are making their young shoots. After they have done growing, watering once or twice a week will be sufficient till the flower-buds again begin to swell.

During the growing season, the plants should be set out and syringed all over the leaves once or twice a-week; but care should be taken not to do this when the sun shines, or at any rate not to set the plants in the sun while they are wet, as the heat of the sun acting on the water will scald the leaves, and make them appear blotched, and partially withered. The roots of Camellias are seldom very strong, and they are very easily injured. Great care should, therefore, be taken when the plants are repotted, not to bruise the roots, or to cut off all that are at all injured. If on turning out the plants previous to repotting, the ball of earth has no white roots appearing on the outside, the earth and decayed roots should be shaken or cleared away, till good roots are seen; and these should be carefully examined, and all the bad parts cut away. The plants should then be repotted in a pot not more than an inch in diameter than the diameter of the ball of earth left round the sound roots; and it should be well drained at the bottom with very small potshreds, or clean gravel.

Small Camellias should not be shifted oftener than once in

two years; and large ones, that is, those above five feet high, not oftener than once in three or four years; but if the earth in the pot appears to have sunk, a little vegetable mould may be laid on the surface. The usual time for shifting Camellias is just when they have done flowering before they are beginning to send out their young shoots. When planted in the free ground in a conservatory, they will require no other care than regular watering, and syringing the leaves once or twice a-week. When planted in the open air, the roots should be carefully protected by straw during frosty weather.

There are some Camellias in the Vauxhall Nursery (Messrs. Chandler's), which have been treated in his manner, and have stood out for several years. The hardiest kinds, and the most suitable for planting in the open air, are the single red, the double red, and the double white. The magnificent Camellia reticulata is also said to be tolerably hardy. The tenderest of the common kinds are the beautiful apple-flowered variety of C. Sasanqua, and the single variety of this species, the flower of which resembles that of the tea-plant. These plants are both of low growth, and ought always to be kept in pots. Camellias are very often infected with insects, particularly a kind of black aphis, the only remedies for which are fumigation and constant syringing. The leaves of Camellias should be always syringed on the under side, as well as on the surface, as they curve inwards a little, and thus afford a shelter to insects, from which it is very difficult to dislodge them. For an account of the new method of grafting the Camellia, now practiced with great success at Knight's Exotic Nursery, King's road, Chelsea, and some other places.

The best collections of Camellias in London are those of
Messrs. Loddiges at Hackney, Messrs. Chandler's at Vauxhall,
and Messrs. Lees at Hammersmith.

Geraniums and Pelargoniums

The beautiful green-house shrubs, which we are accustomed
to call Geraniums, have, in fact, been long separated from
that genus, and formed into a new one called Pelargonium.
The difference is in the shape of the seed vessel; that of the
Pelargonium being like a stork's bill, and that of the Geranium
like a crane's bill. Both are nearly allied to the Touch-me-not:
and when the seed is ripe, the valves of the seed-pod burst
asunder and curl up.

There are almost innumerable species, hybrids, and varieties
of Pelargoniums grown in our green-houses, so mixed up
together by hybridizing that it is very difficult even to class them.
One of the hardiest kinds, which has numerous descendants, is
the Horse-shoe Geranium, Pelargonium zonale: and another, P.
inquinans, is the common scarlet. The rose-scented Geranium,
P. graveolens, and oak-leaved, P. uercifoliu, with their numerous
descendants, the flowers of which are all crimson, striped with
brown so very dark that it looks almost black, are also tolerably
hardy. All the shrubby kinds, which are generally kept in green-
houses require a rich loamy soil, that is, about half very rotten
dung, and half sandy loam, to make them produce fine flowers.
When the flowering season is over, the plants are cut down, and
cuttings made from them.

When these have struck, they are potted in a compost of

Geranium, Erodium

vegetable mould and sand, and kept in this soil till February or March, when they are repotted in rich soil for flowering. Some gardeners throw away the old pants as soon as they have made the cuttings, but others take the old plants out of their pots, and shaking the earth from them, cut in the roots, and repot the plants in smaller pots. Pelargoniums require a great deal of air; and when about to flower they should have a great deal of water, but at other seasons very little. They are killed with the slightest frost; and they are very liable to damp off, if watered too much, and not allowed sufficient air, in winter. Air is, indeed, quite essential to them. The best geranium growers in or near London are Mr. Catleugh of Chelsea, and Mr. Gaines of Battersea.

Heaths

The kinds grown in green-houses are all natives of the Cape of Good Hope, and they are very numerous; but they may be classed under six heads, which are named from the shape of their flowers. These divisions are tubular shaped, ventricose, spreading or salver shaped, with an inflated calyx, globular, and ovate. They all require to be potted high, and to be grown in three parts of peat-earth to one part of fine white sand, or in what is emphatically called heath mould. The fine hair-like roots of the heaths cannot penetrate a stiff loamy soil, and manure would be too gross for their spongioles to take up. The collar of the plants should always be above the soil, as it is very easily rotten by moisture. Heaths require good drainage, and frequent waterings; and though the water should never be allowed to stand in the saucer, the roots should also never be allowed to become quite dry, as, when once withered, they can never be recovered. Heaths also require abundance of free air, and no plants are more injured by being kept in rooms. They should not be shifted oftener than once in three or four years. They are propagated by cuttings taken from the tips of the shoots, and then struck in pure white sand. The pots containing the cuttings should be plunged up to the rim in a hot-bed, and each should be covered with a bell glass. Heaths are easily killed by frost, which acts upon them by splitting, or rather shivering their stems. The best heaths near London are those of Messrs. Rollisson of Tooting; but there are also good collections at Messrs. Henderson's, Pine Apple Place, Lee's, Hammersmith, and Chandler's, Vauxhall.

Verbenas

No family of plants better rewards the care of the cultivator, and none can be more beautiful, than the Verbenas. The old scarlet Verbena melindres, or, as it is frequently called, V. chamaedrifolia, is the most brilliant of all the kinds, though it is one of the most tender: it is a prostrate plant, and when pegged down, it is well adapted for covering a bed in a geometric flower garden, or it may be planted in a vase, or rustic flower-basket, to hand down over the sides.

Verbena Tweediana is an upright growing plant, and though the flowers, which are crimson, are not half so brilliant as those of V. melindres, the plant has the great advantage of being one of the hardiest of all the kinds.

Verbena

V. melindres latifolia, and V. m. splendens are both hardier than their parent, and they unite its brilliant colour, with the upright habit of Tweediana.

V. incisa has pale pink flowers, and an upright habit of growth. It is tolerably hardy, and grows freely, but its flowers have a faded look.

V. Arraniana has an upright habit of growth, and purple flowers, with very dark bluish green leaves. It is very tender, and very apt to be attacked by a kind of aphis, and other insects.

V. pulchellal, V. Aubletia, V. Lambertiii, and V. Sabinii, are prostrate tufted half herbaceous kinds, all hardy.

V. Neillii has lilac flowers, and rather an upright habit of growth; and V. teucroides is a coarse-growing plant, with along spike of what flowers, which turn pink in dying off, that has been much more praised than it deserves. There is also a yellowish kind, V. sulphurea; V. venosa, a very strong-growing species, with purple flowers; and many other species, hybrids, and varieties.

All the Verbenas require to be grown in sand and peat, or heath-mould and to be kept moderately watered; they all strike readily from cuttings or layers; and, indeed, when pegged down, even without any slitting or twisting, most of the shrubby kinds will thrown out roots at every joint. When worm-casts are observed on the surface of the earth in the pot, as will very often be the case, the plant, with its ball of earth entire, may be turned out of the pot, and the worms, which will always be found on the outside of the ball, may be picked off. Worms do considerable injury to plants, especially such as are in pots, by

rupturing the fibres, and impeding the free percolation of the
water, besides giving the surface of the earth in the pot a very
unpleasant appearance.

The flowers of the Verbenas should always be cut off as
soon as they wither. The Lemon plant, Verbena trphylla, now
called Aloysia citriodora, is remarkable for the sweetness of
the odour of its leaves. It is tolerably hardy; but requires great
care in watering; as the leaves will soon curl up and wither if it
has too little, and they will drop off if it has too much water.
The flower has no beauty; and the only recommendation for
the plant is the delightful fragrance of its leaves.

Petunias

Petunias may be raised either from seed or cuttings, as they
seed freely, and strike readily. The first kind introduced was
Petunia nyetanginiflora, which produces a great abundance of
large, white, fragrant flowers; Petunia phoenicea, or violacea,
is another original species, and from these two nearly all the
myriads of hybrids and varieties now found in gardens have
arisen.

These Petunias hybridize freely with each other, and most
of the kinds produce abundance of seed; but P. bicolor is a
distinct species, which does not either mix well with the others,
or seed freely. Petunias may be treated as annuals, and raised on
a slight hot-bed every year from seed; and thus treated, they will
do very well in the open ground, and will come up and flower
abundantly. Treated as green-house plants they are, however, all
shrubby, and will last several years.

When intended to be kept in pots, the seed should be sown on a slight hot-bed in February, and the young plants should be pricked out into very small thumb pots, while they are in the seed leaf. In these pots they should remain either in the frame of the hot-bed, or in a room, or green-house, for about a week or ten days, and they should be then shifted into somewhat larger pots. These shiftings, always into somewhat larger pots, should be repeated six, eight, or ten times, if the plants are wanted to be bushy; and not more than four, if the plants are wished to grow tall.

The busy plants will flower abundantly without any support; but the tall-growing plants, which are suffered to flower in comparatively small pots, must be trained to some kind of frame. When the tall plants appear to be growing too straggling, the extremities of the shoots should be taken off and made into cuttings. Petunias may be grown in any good garden soil; and require no particular attention as to water, &c. In fact, they are, perhaps, the best of all plants for a lady to cultivate; as they will afford a great deal of interest and amusement, with the least possible amount of trouble.

Fuchsias

Fuchsias are another family of plants that may be cultivated with very little trouble. Fuchsia globosa is perhaps the hardiest kind. F. virgata is also tolerably hardy. All the Fuchsias require a light, rich soil, or a mixture of rich sandy loam and peat; and regular watering, as when the outer roots are once withered, either by want of moisture, or by exposure to the direct rays of

the sun, the plant generally dies. For this reason the Fuchsia is
not so well adapted for a window plant as many others. Fuchsia
fulgens differs considerably from the other species, and will not
flower well unless in the open air, and with a sunny exposure.
It is also tuberous rooted, though woody in its stem. It is easily
propagated; and even a leaf taken off without injuring the part
of the petiole which was attached to the stem, has been known
to grow and form a plant. Several handsome hybrids have been
produced, by applying the pollen of F. fulgens to the stigma of
F. globosa, F. conica, and F. grailis. It may here be mentioned,
that whenever hybrids are to be raised, by fertilizing one plant
with the pollen of another, the anthers of the flower that is to
produce the seed should be removed with a pair of scissors
before they burst. The pollen from the other flower which is
to form the hybrid, should be afterwards applied with a camel-
hair pencil to the stigma of the flower which is to produce the
seed; and a bit of that should be tied round the flower-stalk, in
order that the seed-pod may be saved and set apart.

All hybrids may be made in the same manner; but it must
always be remembered that flowers will not hybridize properly,
unless they are naturally nearly allied. Nearly allied to F. fulgens
is the newly introduced F. corymbiflora, which, as Dr. Lindley
very justly observes, casts all the other Fuchsias into the shade.
This magnificent plant is described by Ruiz and Pavon, in the
Flora Peruviana, as growing to the height of a man, and it is
perfectly laden with flowers, which are produced in the same
manner as those of F. fulgens, but far exceeds them, both in
elegance of shape, and brilliance of colour. The tube part of

the flower is a clear bright rose colour, with the tips very much turned back, and the petals thus displayed are of the richest and most brilliant carmine. The species was raised by Mr. Standish, Nurseryman, Bagshot, and it appears likely to be quite as hardy as F. fulgens. The best Fuchsias in the neighbourhood of London are those of Mr. Standish at Bagshot, but some very handsome varieties have bene raised by Mr. Groom of Walworth.

Calceolarias

Perhaps no plants have ever been hybridized more extensively than these. The principal parents of the numerous and splendid plants that we are continually seeing produced, are C. corymbosa, and C. arachnoidea, the one a yellow, and the other purple flower; but there are many other species that have been crossed and re-crossed with these, so as to form a very great variety. C. bicolor, with pale yellow-and-white flowers, and C. crenatiflora, with spotted flowers, have also been the parents of some very fine hybrids and varieties. All the calceolarias require rather a rich soil, and the usual compost is two parts of thoroughly rotten dung, one part of leaf mould, or old turf, and one part of white sand. The ingredients of this compost should be well mixed together, and broken fine, but not sifted. They also require plenty of water, and abundance of light and air; and they will all flower best when allowed plenty of room for their roots. They are, however, very subject to be attacked by a kind of aphis: and when kept in pots, they should be frequently syringed. The best Calceolarias, near London, are those of Mr. Catleugh at Chelsea.

Myrtles

Myrtles should be grown in a soil composed of peat and loam, in which the former predominates; they should be regularly watered, and frequently syringed Some persons nip off the tips of the young shoots, to make the plants grown bushy; and though it has this effect, it is a bad practice with the flowering kinds, as it prevents them from producing flowers. A better plan is to make cuttings, and first to plant them in very small pots, gradually changing them into larger ones, till the plants have acquired a bushy habit of growth.

Mimulus

Some of the plants belonging to this genus are very handsome, particularly the hybrids raised by the nurserymen from M. cardinalis, M. roseus, M. luteus, and M. gattatus. These species are all herbaceous, and all natives of South America, Mexico, and California. They are all nearly hardy, and though generally grown in a green-house, they will stand quite well in the open air, dying down to the ground in winter, but sending up fresh and very vigorous shoots in spring. When these plants are grown in the open ground it should be in a shady moist situation; and when they are kept in pots, they should always stand in saucers half full of water. This water should, however, be changed every day, and when given to the plants it should always be as nearly as possible of the same temperature as themselves.

The little musk plant, Mimulus moschata, requires the same treatment as its more showy brethren. As all the species of Mimulus have been found in their native habitats growing in

Mimulus

coarse sand or gravel on the brink of a river, this kind of soil should be chosen for them in pots; and the soil in which they are grown can hardly be too poor, provided they have abundance of water. In Chili, the inhabitants eat the leaves as a kind of vegetable. The shrubby kinds of Mimulus, viz., the common monkey plant, M. luteus, and the scarlet-flowered species, M. puniceus, are now considered to belong to a new genus called Diplacus. They are both natives of California; and in their treatment they should be considered as green-house plants, and have rather a better soil, and less water, than the true kinds of Mimulus.

Hydrangea Hortensia

Hydrangea Hortensia is another plant that, when grown in a pot, requires to have the saucer kept half full of water. There are several species, most of which are hardy shrubs, but Hydrangea Hortensia, the kind usually called the Hydrangea, is a native of China and only half hardy, though it will live in the open air in sheltered situations, or with a very slight protection. This plant was named Hortensia by the botanist Commerson in compliment to Madame Hortense Lapeaute, the wife of a French watch-maker. The Hydrangea, should be grown in a rich loamy soil, and pruned every year; all the old wood being cut out, so that the wood which is to produce the flower shoots should never be more than two or at most three years old.

Cuttings strike readily at any season when the plant is in a growing state; if put into a rich soil and kept moist, they will root in a fortnight, and flower in a month. The flowers of the Hydrangea, though generally pink, are sometimes blue; and the art of making them blue at pleasure, has long been a desideratum among gardeners. A great number of recipes for this purpose have been given in gardening books, but though all of them are occasionally successful, none of them will ensure success. Sometimes transplanting Hydrangeas that have been grown in loam into peat, will have the desired effect; and at others, watering with water in which iron has been steeped will change the colour of the flowers. The ferruginous yellow loams of Hampstead Heath and Stanmore Common are almost always efficacious, but even these have been know sometimes to fail. All that is known with certainty is, that a the change of colour is only a variation, and not permanent, as cuttings taken from a blue Hydrangea, and planted in common soil, almost always produce pink flowers.

Mesembryanthemums
There are very few things in gardening respecting which gardeners appear more to disagree than in the treatment of succulent plants; particularly of the Mesembryanthemums, which are mostly natives of the sandy plains near the Cape of Good Hope, where they are subjected to alternate seasons of extreme wet and extreme dryness. Cultivators attempting to imitate these peculiarities, have grown these succulent plants in poor sandy soil, and kept them entirely without water at one season, while they have been inundated with it at another; but the fact is, that when we attempt to imitate nature, we should remember that the attempt is useless, unless we can do so in

every particular; and also that the plants we have to cultivate, have been nursed up into so very artificial a state, that if they were transplanted to their native plains they would probably perish, like a poor Canary bird, which a mistaken philanthropy has turned out of the cage in which it has long lived.

For this reason, we must adopt the mode of treating succulents, which the best gardeners find most successful, without troubling ourselves to discover why it is so different from the natural habit of the plants. This mode of treatment is, then, to grow the plants in a rich loamy soil, kept open, as it is called, by the addition of lime rubbish; and to give the plants water all the year, but more moderately when they are in a dormant, than when they are in a growing state. They should also have as much air and light as possible. The water should never be suffered to stand in the saucer of any succulent plant; but it should be given regularly, diminishing the quantity a little every day as the season for rest approaches. If the water be suddenly stopped, the leaves of the plants will shrink and become flaccid, and when this is the case, the plant generally dies. A deficiency of air on the other hand will cause the plant to damp off. All Mesembryanthemums are very soon affected by frost; but will thrive in the open air in summer.

The Cacti

The Cacti, which are also succulent plants, are arranged in several quite distinct groups, which require different treatment. The first of these comprises the various kinds of tree Cereus, which have long slender stems, thirty or forty feet high, without either branches or leaves. These singular looking plants grow on the summit of the mountains of Brazil, in a poor, dry, stony soil, and exposed on every side to the cold breezes of the lofty regions they inhabit. In England, they should be kept in only green-house heat, even in winter; and they should have abundance of light and air; while they should be grown in pots well drained with cinders, and filled up with a mixture of loam, and pounded brick and lime rubbish.

The Mammalarias and Echinocacti, forming the group called the Porcupine Cacti, grown in the valleys of the temperate regions, generally in loamy soil, and among thick short grass, passing half their year in continual rain. The Opuntias and Pereskias are found on almost barren hills; the Opuntia, which is always known by its flat oval leaves or rather stems, and its prickly but eatable fruit, growing in narrow chinks among rocks where there does not appear sufficient soil to nourish a blade of grass. In some cases these plants grow nearly to the verge of a perpetual snow. The Pereskias, which have leaves distinct from their stems, grow in similar situations, and require only a moderate degree of heat; but the Melocacti and the Rhipsalis are only found in the hottest part of the tropics.

All the Cacti should be grown in pots well drained with cinders, and in soil composed of a little sandy loam mixed with lime rubbish. They should all be watered regularly and abundantly when they are growing, or coming into flower, and kept nearly dry during their season of repose; and they all enjoy having their pots plunged in a slight hot-bed, which makes them throw out abundance of roots.

The Australian plants

The Australian plants, of which so many beautiful kinds have
been introduced within the last few years, should nearly all be
grown in a mixture of sand and peat; and they should have their
pots filled one-third with potshreds. They all require abundance
of water, but they will all perish if water be retained about their
roots. Most of the Australian plants are very tenacious of life,
and if cut down when they appear dead, they will generally
spring up again from the collar of the root.

Climbing plants

The principal climbing plants grown in pots are the Maurandyas,
the Lophospermums, the Passion-flowers, the Rhodochiton,
the Ecremocarpus, or Calempelis, the Imomaeas, and the
Cobaea. There are, however, several others, all of which are
very handsome. The greater part of these require a rich light
soil to make them grow rapidly, and to be planted in the ground
of the conservatory. The Bignonias or Tecomas should be
grown in equal parts of loam and peat,; and this compost will
suit the Polygalas, and other showy climbers. The Sollyas and
Billiardieras should be grown in peat and frequently syringed
to keep off the green fly. The Thunbergias are very liable to
be attacked by the red spider. Many of the shrubby climbers
may be treated as annuals, and raised from seed every year in
January, and planted out in June; but they do still better treated
as biennials, and sown one year to flower the next.

All the most beautiful hot-house climbers, such as the
Allamanda cathartica, the Impomaea Horsfalliae, Peraea

volubilis, &c., may be grown in the open air, by keeping their roots in heat; that is to say, if the roots are grown in a stove, or in a pit heated by hot water or flues to stove-heat, the stems may be brought through some opening purposely contrived, and twined over a trellis in the open garden. A very striking effect may be thus produced by having a bed heated by hot-water pipes concealed under ground, at the foot of a veranda, over which these beautiful tropical climbers may be trained.

Gladiolus